Barcelona

SUMARIO

Contents

Background

Modernism

Exploring the city

Main museums

Other museums and sights of interest

Directory

Index

On the waterfront between the Montjuïc and Tibidabo mountains, Barcelona, economic and political capital of Cataluyna, is most certainly one of the most attractive and cosmopolitan cities in Spain. The modern and elegant avenues of the Eixample and la Vila Olímpica complement the charming narrow streets of the old quarters.
A Mediterranean port city, Barcelona is characterised by its great monuments and many winding streets as well as the intense cultural opportunities and nightlife, all of which attract visitors from around the world to this enchanting city. It is one of those rare places where the traditional and the contemporary are in harmony, where art and history abound and cultural is part of daily life.
All of your senses will be awakened in Barcelona. Strolling through town, you will discover surprising modernist buildings, magnificent museums and contemporary art foundations, majestic Gothic churches, spaces where contemporary designs shines at its best, gorgeous perspectives and captivating neighbourhoods.

J. Malburet/MICHELIN

Introduction

Parc Güell

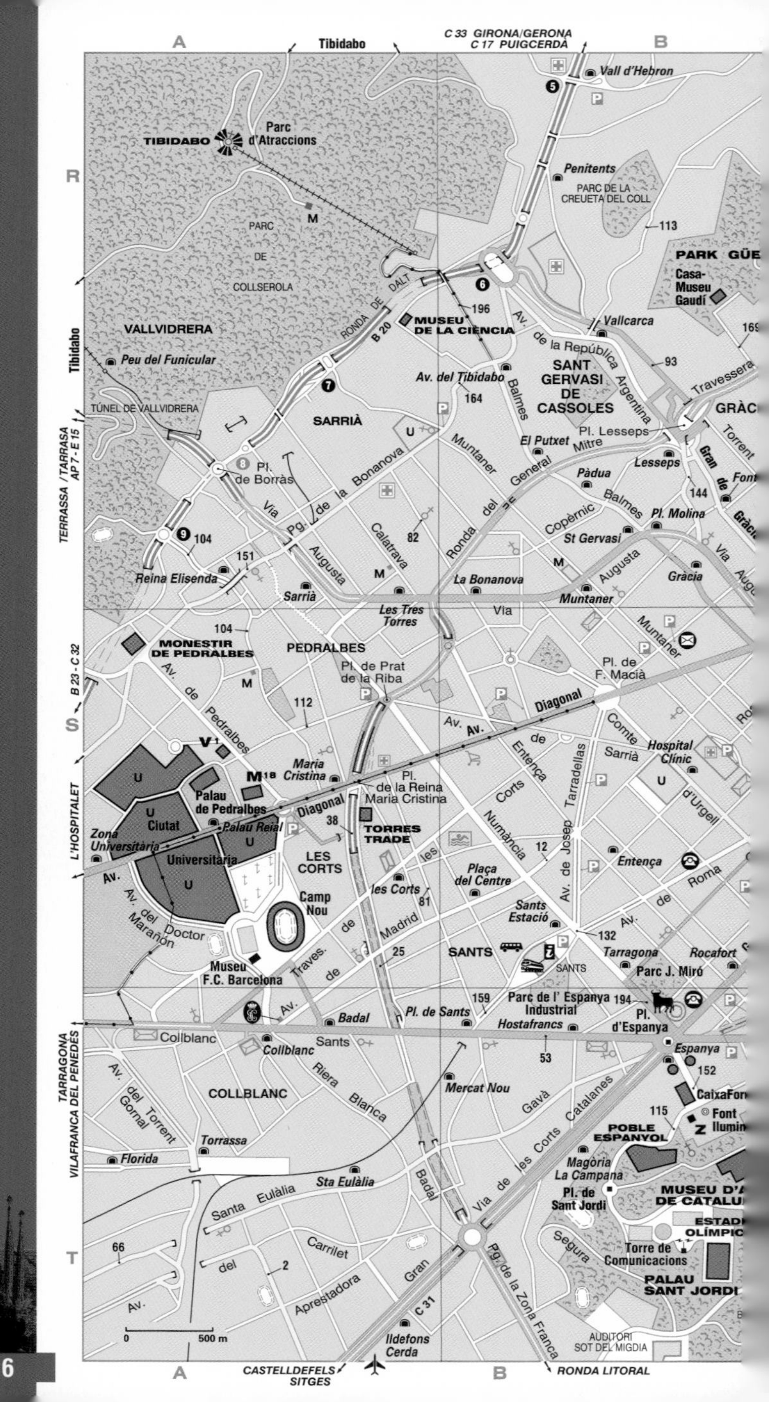
A
B
Tibidabo
C 33 GIRONA/GERONA
C 17 PUIGCERDÀ
R
S
T
Vall d'Hebron
TIBIDABO
Parc d'Atraccions
Penitents
PARC DE LA CREUETA DEL COLL
PARC DE COLLSEROLA
PARK GÜE
Casa-Museu Gaudí
VALLVIDRERA
Peu del Funicular
RONDA DE DALT
B 20
MUSEU DE LA CIÈNCIA
Vallcarca
Av. de la República Argentina
Av. del Tibidabo
SANT GERVASI DE CASSOLES
Travessera
GRÀCI
TÚNEL DE VALLVIDRERA
SARRIÀ
Balmes
El Putxet
Pl. Lesseps
Mitre
Lesseps
Torrent
Pl. de Borràs
Pg. de la Bonanova
Muntaner
Ronda del General
Pàdua
Gran de Gràcia
Via Augusta
Calatrava
Copèrnic
Pl. Molina
St Gervasi
Reina Elisenda
Sarrià
La Bonanova
Muntaner
Gràcia
Les Tres Torres
Via
MONESTIR DE PEDRALBES
PEDRALBES
Pl. de Prat de la Riba
Pl. de F. Macià
Av. de Pedralbes
Av. Diagonal
Comte de Sarrià
Av. de Entença
Hospital Clínic
Maria Cristina
Palau de Pedralbes
Pl. de la Reina Maria Cristina
Corts
Tarradellas
d'Urgell
Zona Universitària
Ciutat Universitaria
Palau Reial
Diagonal
TORRES TRADE
Numància
LES CORTS
les
Plaça del Centre
Entença
Av. de Josep
Roma
Av.
Av. del Doctor Marañón
Camp Nou
les Corts
Sants Estació
Av. de Roma
Madrid
Traves. de
Museu F.C. Barcelona
SANTS
Tarragona
Rocafort
Parc J. Miró
Parc de l' Espanya Industrial
Pl. d'Espanya
Badal
Pl. de Sants
Hostafrancs
Collblanc
Sants
Espanya
COLLBLANC
Riera Blanca
Mercat Nou
Gavà
Via de les Corts Catalanes
CaixaFor
POBLE ESPANYOL
Font Illumin
Torrassa
Florida
Sta Eulàlia
Magòria La Campana
Pl. de Sant Jordi
MUSEU D'A DE CATALU
ESTAD OLÍMPIC
Santa Eulàlia
Carrilet
del
Aprestadora
Gran
C 31
Segura
Pg. de la Zona Franca
Torre de Comunicacions
PALAU SANT JORDI
Ildefons Cerdà
AUDITORI SOT DEL MIGDIA
0
500 m
TERRASSA / TARRASA AP 7 - E 15
B 23 - C 32
L'HOSPITALET
TARRAGONA VILAFRANCA DEL PENEDÈS
CASTELLDEFELS SITGES
RONDA LITORAL

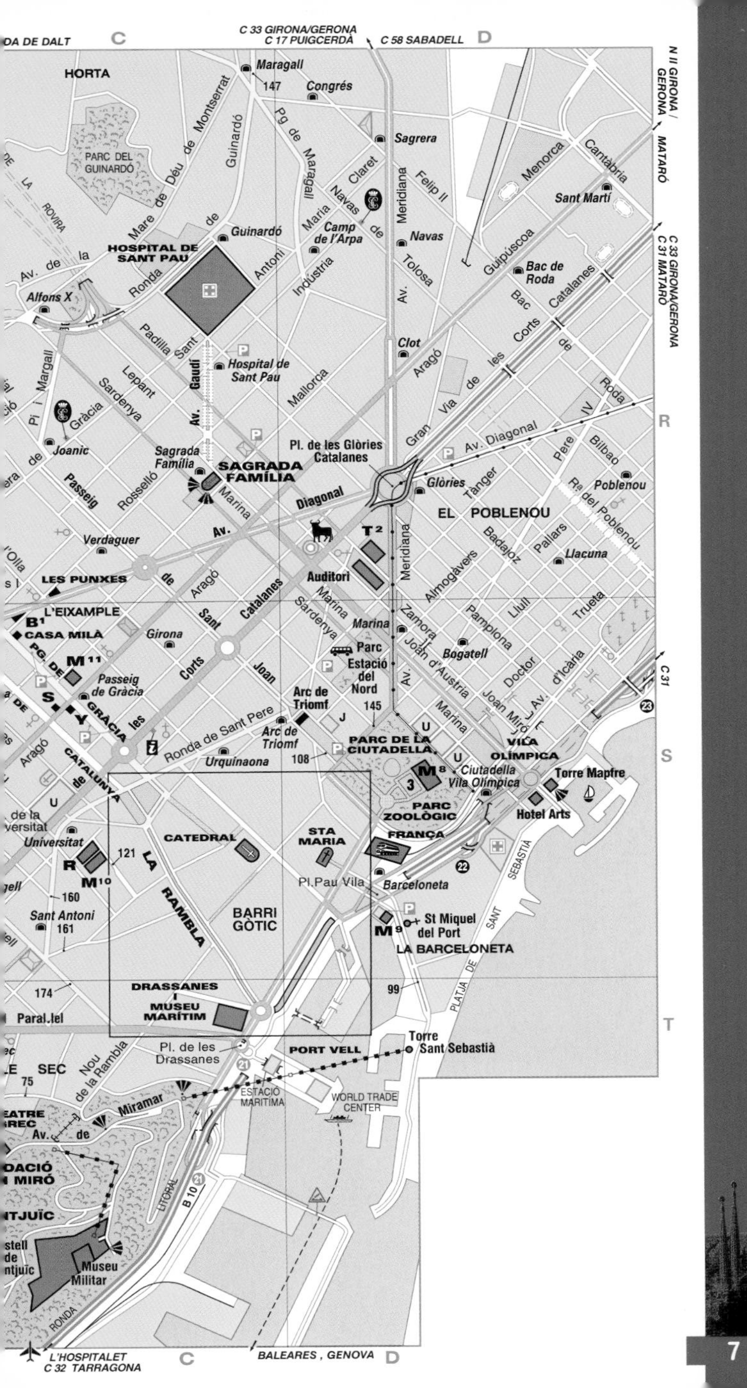
C 33 GIRONA/GERONA
C 17 PUIGCERDÀ
C 58 SABADELL
C
D
HORTA
Maragall
147
Congrés
PARC DEL GUINARDÓ
Mare de Déu de Montserrat
Guinardó
Pg de Maragall
Sagrera
Claret
Felip II
Menorca
Cantàbria
N II GIRONA / GERONA
MATARÓ
Sant Martí
Navas
Meridiana
Camp de l'Arpa
Guinardó
HOSPITAL DE SANT PAU
Ronda
Antoni
Maria
Indústria
Navas
Tolosa
Guipúscoa
Bac de Roda
C 33 GIRONA/GERONA
C 31 MATARÓ
Av. de la
Alfons X
Padilla
Sant
Hospital de Sant Pau
Clot
Aragó
Corts
Catalanes
Bac
de
Pi i Margall
Lepant
Sardenya
Av. Gaudí
Mallorca
Gran Via de les
Roda
IV
Gràcia
Joanic
Sagrada Família
SAGRADA FAMÍLIA
Pl. de les Glòries Catalanes
Av. Diagonal
Pere
Bilbao
R
Passeig
Rosselló
Marina
Diagonal
Glòries
Tànger
Ra del Poblenou
Poblenou
EL POBLENOU
Av.
T²
Badajoz
Pallars
Llacuna
Verdaguer
LES PUNXES
de
Aragó
Auditori
Meridiana
Almogàvers
L'EIXAMPLE
B¹
CASA MILÀ
Girona
Sant
Catalanes
Marina
Sardenya
Marina
Zamora
Pamplona
Llull
Trueta
PG. DE
M¹¹
Passeig de Gràcia
GRÀCIA
Corts
Joan
Parc Estació del Nord
Joan d'Àustria
Bogatell
Doctor
d'Icària
C 31
les
Arc de Triomf
145
J
Av.
Marina
Joan Miró
Av.
23
Ronda de Sant Pere
Arc de Triomf
PARC DE LA CIUTADELLA
U
VILA OLÍMPICA
Aragó
CATALUNYA
de
Urquinaona
108
M⁸
3
Ciutadella Vila Olímpica
Torre Mapfre
S
U
de la versitat
Universitat
CATEDRAL
STA MARIA
PARC ZOOLÒGIC
FRANÇA
Hotel Arts
121
LA RAMBLA
R
M¹⁰
Pl.Pau Vila
Barceloneta
22
SEBASTIÀ
160
Sant Antoni
161
BARRI GÒTIC
M⁹
St Miquel del Port
LA BARCELONETA
SANT
DE
PLATJA
174
DRASSANES I MUSEU MARÍTIM
99
Paral.lel
T
Pl. de les Drassanes
Nou de la Rambla
PORT VELL
Torre Sant Sebastià
LE SEC
75
21
ESTACIÓ MARÍTIMA
WORLD TRADE CENTER
Miramar
Av. de
LITORAL
B 10
21
Museu Militar
RONDA
L'HOSPITALET
C 32 TARRAGONA
BALEARES, GENOVA
C
D

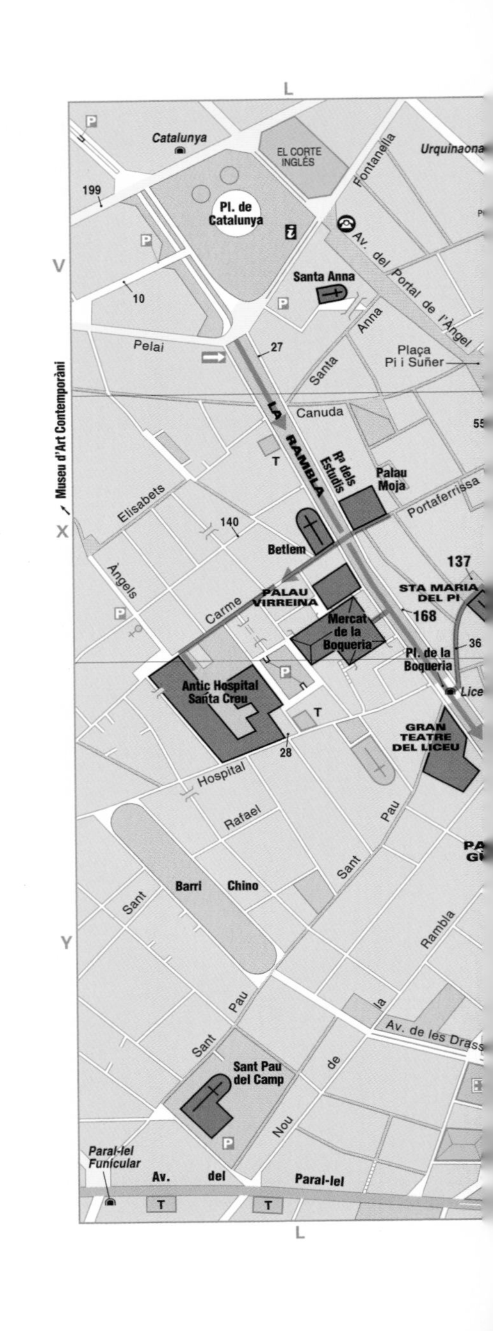
L
Catalunya
EL CORTE INGLÉS
Fontanella
Urquinaona
199
Pl. de Catalunya
Av. del Portal de l'Àngel
V
Santa Anna
10
Anna
Santa
Pelai
27
Plaça Pi i Suñer
LA RAMBLA
Canuda
Museu d'Art Contemporàni
T
Rª dels Estudis
Palau Moja
Portaferrissa
Elisabets
140
X
Betlem
137
Àngels
PALAU VIRREINA
STA MARIA DEL PI
Carme
Mercat de la Boqueria
168
36
Pl. de la Boqueria
Antic Hospital Santa Creu
GRAN TEATRE DEL LICEU
T
28
Hospital
Rafael
Pau
Sant
Barri Chino
Sant
Rambla
Y
Pau
la
Av. de les Drass
Sant
Sant Pau del Camp
de
Nou
Paral-lel Funicular
Av. del Paral-lel
T
T
L

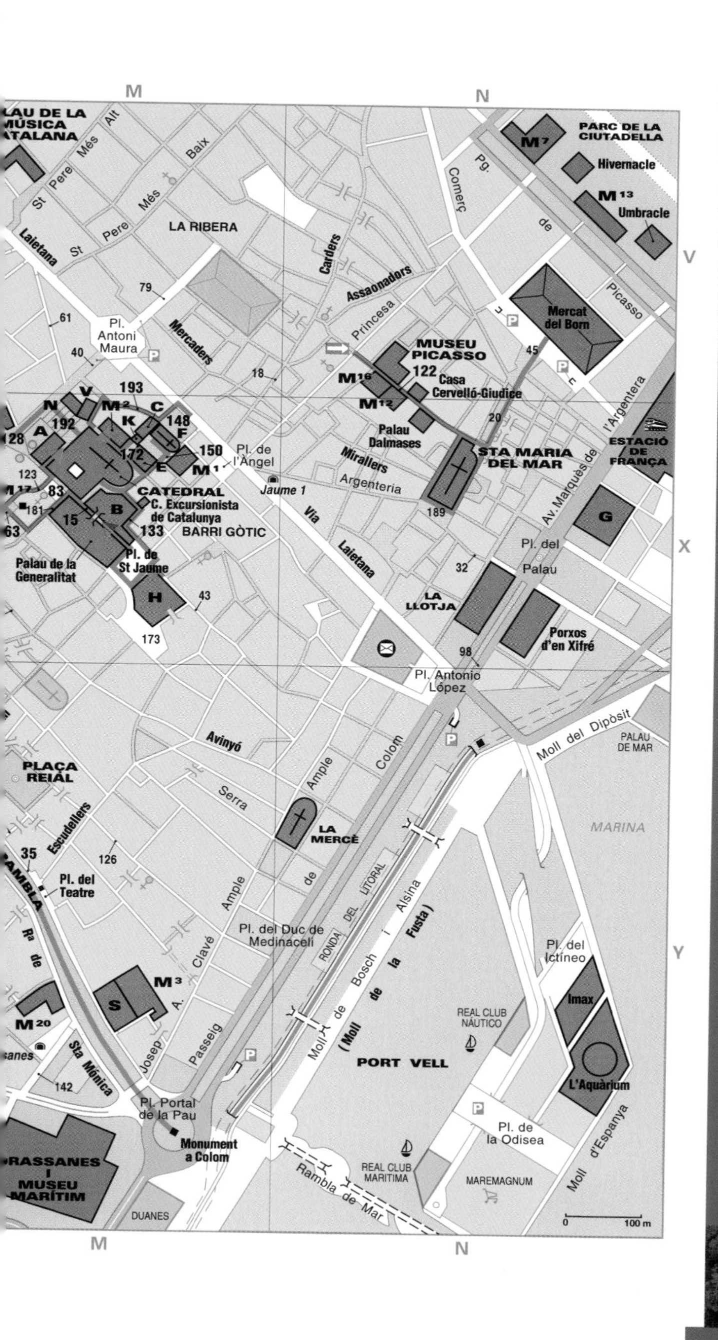
M
N
PARC DE LA CIUTADELLA
Hivernacle
Umbracle
LA RIBERA
Carders
Assaonadors
Princesa
Mercaders
Pl. Antoni Maura
MUSEU PICASSO
Casa Cervelló-Giudice
Palau Dalmases
Mercat del Born
Picasso
Pg. de Comerç
STA MARIA DEL MAR
Miralls
Argenteria
Av. Marquès de l'Argentera
ESTACIÓ DE FRANÇA
CATEDRAL
C. Excursionista de Catalunya
BARRI GÒTIC
Pl. de l'Àngel
Jaume 1
Via Laietana
Palau de la Generalitat
Pl. de St Jaume
Pl. del Palau
LA LLOTJA
Porxos d'en Xifré
Pl. Antonio López
Moll del Dipòsit
PALAU DE MAR
Avinyó
PLAÇA REIAL
Serra
Ample
Colom
LA MERCÈ
MARINA
Escudellers
Pl. del Teatre
Pl. del Duc de Medinaceli
RONDA DEL LITORAL
Moll de Bosch i Alsina
(Moll de la Fusta)
Pl. del Ictíneo
Imax
REAL CLUB NÁUTICO
PORT VELL
L'Aquàrium
Moll d'Espanya
Pl. de la Odisea
Passeig Josep A. Clavé
Sta Mònica
Pl. Portal de la Pau
Monument a Colom
REAL CLUB MARITIMA
MAREMAGNUM
Rambla de Mar
DUANES
0 100 m
V
X
Y

Monument	Grid	Key
Ajuntament	MX	**H**
Capella Santa Agata	MX	**F**
Casa de la Canonja	MX	**V**
Casa de l'Ardiaca	MX	**A**
Casa dels Canonges	MX	**B**
Casa Quadras	CS	**B**^{1}
Casas : Amatlier, Batlió, Bonet, Morera, Mulleras	CS	**Y**
Castell dels Tres Dragons (Museu de Zoologia)	NV	**M**^{7}
Centre de Cultura Contemporàna de Barcelona (Centre d'Estudis i de Recurses Culturals)	CS	**R**
Collegi d'Arquitectes	MX	**L**
Convento de Santa Mònica	MY	**M**^{20}
Duana Nova	NX	**G**
Fundació Antoni Tàpies	CS	**S**
Galería olímpica	BT	**M**^{14}
Mirádor del Rei Martí	MX	**K**
Museu Barbier-Mueller d'Art Precolombi	NVX	**M**^{12}
Museu d'Arqueològia de Catalunya	CT	**M**^{5}
Museu d'Art Contemporàni	CS	**M**^{10}
Museu d'Art Modern	DS	**M**^{8}
Museu de Cera	MY	**M**^{3}
Museu de Geología	NV	**M**^{13}
Museu del Calçat	MX	**M**^{17}
Museu dels Carrosses	AS	**M**^{18}
Museu d'Història de Catalunya	DS	**M**^{9}
Museu d'Història de la Ciutat	MX	**M**^{1}
Museu Egipci de Barcelona	CS	**M**^{11}
Museu Etnológic	BT	**M**^{15}
Museu Frederic Marès	MX	**M**^{2}
Palau del Lloctinent	MX	**E**
Palau del Marquès de Llió (Museu Tèxtil i de la Indumentària)	NV	**M**^{16}
Palau Marc	MY	**S**
Pavelló Güell	AS	**V**^{1}
Pavelló Mies van der Rohe	BT	**Z**
Pia Almoina	MX	**N**
Saló del Tinell	MX	**C**
Teatre Nacional de Catalunya	DR	**T**^{2}

eto/TOURISME DE LA CATALOGNE

Bac de Roda Bridge, S. Calatrava

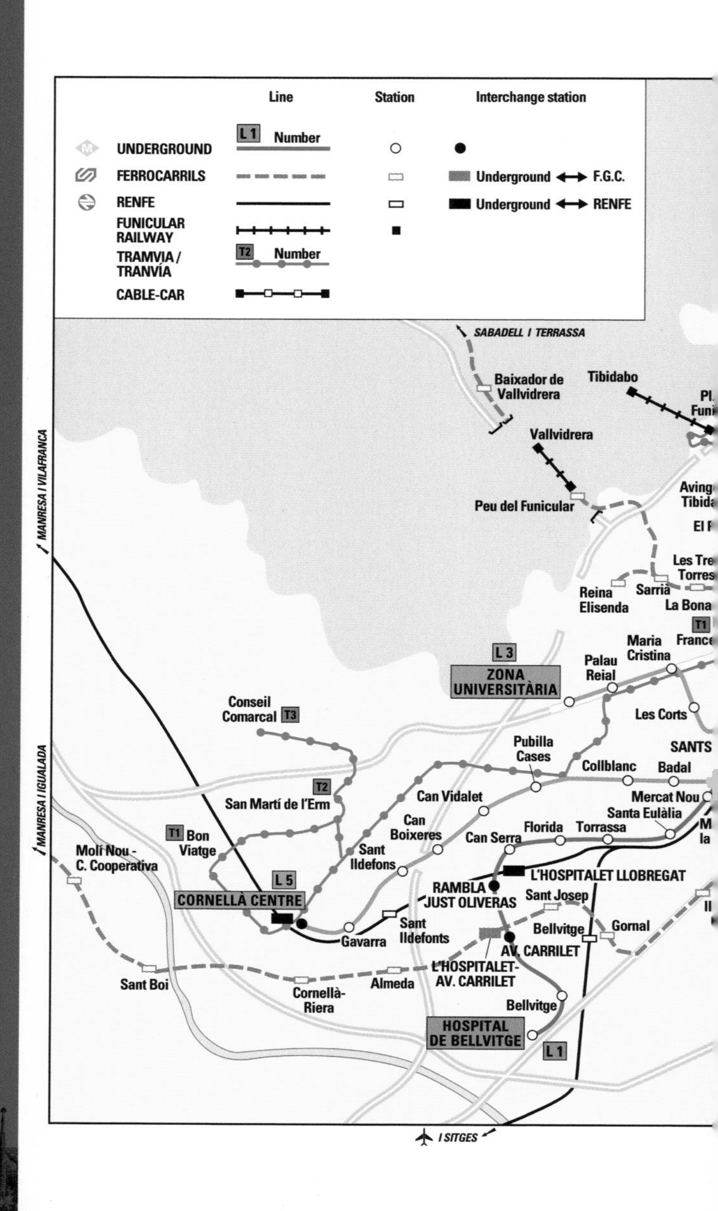

Line
Station
Interchange station
UNDERGROUND
L 1 Number
FERROCARRILS
Underground ↔ F.G.C.
RENFE
Underground ↔ RENFE
FUNICULAR RAILWAY
TRAMVIA / TRANVÍA
T2 Number
CABLE-CAR
SABADELL I TERRASSA
Baixador de Vallvidrera
Tibidabo
Vallvidrera
Peu del Funicular
MANRESA I VILAFRANCA
MANRESA I IGUALADA
Reina Elisenda
Sarrià
La Bona
Les Corts
L 3
ZONA UNIVERSITÀRIA
Palau Reial
Maria Cristina
Conseil Comarcal
T3
Pubilla Cases
SANTS
Collblanc
Badal
T2
San Martí de l'Erm
Can Vidalet
Mercat Nou
Santa Eulàlia
Can Boixeres
Florida
Torrassa
Can Serra
T1 Bon Viatge
Molí Nou - C. Cooperativa
Sant Ildefons
L'HOSPITALET LLOBREGAT
L 5
CORNELLÀ CENTRE
RAMBLA JUST OLIVERAS
Sant Josep
Gavarra
Sant Ildefonts
Bellvitge
Gornal
AV. CARRILET
L'HOSPITALET-AV. CARRILET
Sant Boi
Cornellà-Riera
Almeda
Bellvitge
HOSPITAL DE BELLVITGE
L 1
I SITGES

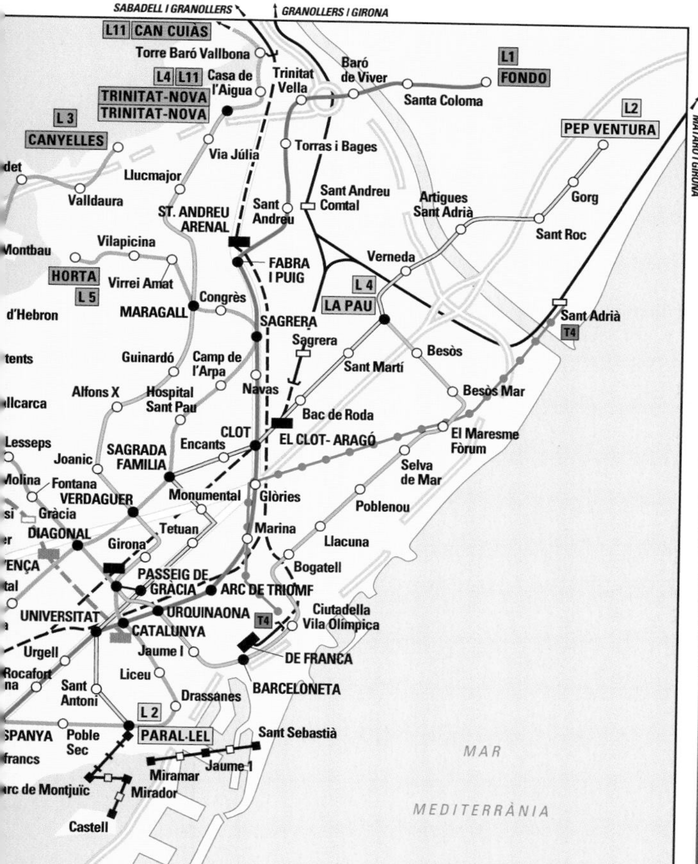

SABADELL I GRANOLLERS
GRANOLLERS I GIRONA
L11 CAN CUIÀS
Torre Baró Vallbona
L1
FONDO
Baró de Viver
L4 L11 Casa de l'Aigua
Trinitat Vella
TRINITAT-NOVA
TRINITAT-NOVA
Santa Coloma
L2
PEP VENTURA
MATARÓ I GIRONA
L 3
CANYELLES
Torras i Bages
Via Júlia
det
Llucmajor
Valldaura
Sant Andreu Comtal
Gorg
Artigues Sant Adrià
Sant Andreu
ST. ANDREU ARENAL
Sant Roc
Vilapicina
Montbau
FABRA I PUIG
Verneda
HORTA
Virrei Amat
L 5
L 4
LA PAU
Congrès
MARAGALL
d'Hebron
SAGRERA
Sant Adrià
T4
Sagrera
tents
Guinardó
Camp de l'Arpa
Besòs
Sant Martí
Alfons X
Hospital Sant Pau
Navas
Besòs Mar
llcarca
Bac de Roda
CLOT
Lesseps
Encants
EL CLOT- ARAGÓ
El Maresme Fòrum
SAGRADA FAMILIA
Joanic
Selva de Mar
Molina
Fontana
VERDAGUER
Monumental
Glòries
Poblenou
si
Gràcia
r
DIAGONAL
Tetuan
Marina
Llacuna
ENÇA
Girona
tal
PASSEIG DE GRÀCIA
Bogatell
ARC DE TRIOMF
UNIVERSITAT
URQUINAONA
Ciutadella Vila Olímpica
T4
CATALUNYA
Urgell
Jaume I
DE FRANCA
Rocafort
na
Liceu
Sant Antoni
Drassanes
BARCELONETA
L 2
SPANYA
PARAL·LEL
Poble Sec
Sant Sebastià
francs
MAR
Miramar
Jaume 1
rc de Montjuïc
Mirador
MEDITERRÀNIA
Castell

Population: 1 681 132. Michelin map 574 H 36 – Michelin City Plans Barcelona 40, 41 and 2040 – Catalunya (Barcelona)

The capital of Cataluyna is one of the leading ports in the Mediterranean. This great maritime city has remained very human in scale. The climate is mild, with average temperatures in winter ranging from 10-13°C (50-55°F) and in summer from 24-25°C (75-77°F).

Barcelona is easy to reach by road, rail, air or sea. It is the hub of an important road network: the AP 7 motorway runs along the Mediterranean coast from Murcia to the French border, passing through Girona; the A 19 heads to the resorts north of the city; the A 16 continues south to Tarragona; while the A 18 veers inland towards Manresa (59km/37mi NE). The El Prat airport is located 12km/7mi south of the city centre. The C 32 runs along the coast from Maresma, linking Barcelona and Tarragona. The C 16 goes as far as Manresa (59km/35mi NE) and the C 17 will carry you to Vic.

i *Paseo de Gràcia 107 (Palau Robert), 08008 Barcelona, ☎ 93 238 40 00; Plaça Catalunya 17, 08002 Barcelona, ☎ 906 30 12 82. www.barcelonaturisme.com Estació Sants, 08015 Barcelona; ☎ 93 491 44 31.*

. Malburet/MICHELIN

Location

J. Malburet/MICHELIN

Background

Cathedral

Barcelona past and present

Origins

Although mythology attributes the origins of Barcelona to Hercules, the city was in fact a Roman colony founded under the reign of the emperor Augustus (1C BC), and known at that time as **Barcino**, a Latin transformation of the Iberian name, Barkeno. It was then a modest village set on a low hill, later to be called "Mons Taber". Today, this hill is in the centre of town. Before the Romans, the region was occupied by Iberians, who lived in hamlets dotting the plain between Besòs and Llobregat. Very little is known about these early inhabitants and their livelihoods. Attracted by the proximity of the sea and the mild climate, many former Roman soldiers settled in the colony and it grew prosperous. The ruins of the 4C ramparts are the main reminder of the Roman period.

From Carolingian rule to autonomy

After a brief period of Moorish domination, Barjel-nah, as the Moors called the city, was seen as a prime objective of the Carolingian Franks. They gained control of the city in 801 and appointed a count to establish Río Ebro on the edge of Cataluyna as the southern limit of their power and a barrier to Moorish progression northward. By the mid-10C, Carolingian domination became weaker and the county dynasties, arising from native lineages, often broke their bonds of vassalage and looked for their own sense of identity. Wilfred the Hairy (Guifré el Pelós) – according to legend, he was born as hairy as a troll, with hair on the soles of his feet, and grew hairier with every passing day – established Barcelona's ruling dynasty. In 988, his successor Count Borrell II *(Guifré II Borrell)* demanded help from the Frankish court to rebuild the city and defend his lands. His appeal unanswered, Borrell II withdrew his loyalty to the Frankish monarch, leading to de facto independence. From that time forth, the Catalan counts ruled with complete sovereignty over their lands.

A period of wealth and splendour followed: the cathedral, the Episcopal palace and the Pía Almoina were built on a basic Romanesque plan unmistakably influenced by Moorish and French architecture, creating a unique new style in the region.

With Ramon Berenguer IV, the counts of Barcelona were transformed into kings, settling the crown firmly on this region of prime political and economic importance. The 13C was the beginning of a period of great prosperity, and Barcelona developed strong

commercial ties. Ships carrying goods from the region dominated traffic in the western reaches of the Mediterranean. Merchants traded with far-off lands, earning great profits and becoming the wealthiest of the city's denizens.
The power and authority of the city, the centre of political activity in Aragon, was soon reflected in its splendid architectural achievements. From the remains of Roman monuments rose austere Gothic buildings with very little Mudéjar influence. Over the centuries, the city forged its own personality, created autonomous government institutions (Consell de Cent, Generalitat). The Barri Gòtic was the neighbourhood where civil and religious authorities tended to build and work, making the district the symbol of the city's prosperity.
Under the reign of the Catholic Kings, the Court left Barcelona and the city entered into a period of decline. The discovery of the New World shifted the focus of trade from the Mediterranean to the Atlantic and Barcelona was left behind.

The War of the Spanish Succession

On September 11, 1714, after desperate resistance, Barcelona surrendered to the troops of the new Bourbon king of Spain, Philip V. The capture of the city ended the war of Succession, during which Cataluyna had supported the Archduke of Austria against Philip of Anjou. The assault on Barcelona was a hard blow and the consequences of surrender spelled out the loss of political autonomy for the city. The Generalitat and the Consell de Cent were dissolved; the legal and constitutional framework was dismantled; the Catalan language was prohibited in schools and in the courts of law. The district of Barceloneta was created at this time, and, with an aim to discouraging

J. Malburet/MICHELIN

La Rambla

or quelling rebellion, Montjuïc was fortified and the citadel built. Local inhabitants were forbidden from building more that 2km/1mi outside the city walls – in other words, beyond the reach of canon fired from the citadel. Nonetheless, the century saw unprecedented demographic and economic growth. By the end of the 18C, the population had tripled in number. A new industrial wave based on the production and export of cotton items carried Barcelona once again to the forefront of the Iberian economy.

From the industrial city to the city of today

Barcelona underwent deep changes during the 18-19C industrial revolution. During this period, some of the city's most emblematic districts (la Rambla and Barceloneta) took on their modern appearance. A period of strong growth in both the economy and the population made it necessary to demolish the ramparts (1854) and enabled a new process of urban planning to be implemented, the **Cerdà Plan**. Thus the city was transformed into a dynamic metropolitan centre. The city limits were extended to include former townships on the periphery, now the neighbourhoods of Gràcia, Sants, Horta, Sarrià, Les Corts, Sant Andreu de Palomar and Sant Martí de Provençals.
The **International Exhibition of 1888** brought the Modernist architecture of Barcelona, favoured by the bourgeoisie and the town planners, into the public eye. As the century waned, anarchist movements flourished with the development of class conflict between the bourgeoisie and the industrial workers. In 1929, a new **International Exhibition** brought a breath of hope to the city, but generally the period leading up to the Spanish Civil War (1036-1939) was punctuated by unrest. Barcelona was one of the cities where post-war repression was especially harsh. In spite of this, the 1950's were prosperous and the political and cultural context eased the transition to democracy. The recovery of its institutions and autonomy helped Barcelona to reassume its role as an administrative and cultural capital. The celebration of the **1992 Olympic Games** encouraged the development of major urban projects (waterfront renewal, restoration in the old town and MontJuïc, construction of a ring-road, etc) and also fostered cultural initiatives (Centre for Contemporary Culture, refurbishing of the Museum of Catalan Art, the Barcelona Museum of Contemporary Art, new university buildings, to cite just a few examples).
More recently, the **Universal Forum of Cultures,** held from May-September 2004, hosting exhibits, debates, performances and more, brought new life to the maritime zone of Sant Adrià del Besòs.

ouret/MICHELIN

ntigua Casa Figueres

Districts of Barcelona

Barcelona's past is still present in its many neighbourhoods, or *barrins*. Once separate villages, often centuries-old, they have been absorbed by urban expansion under the Cerdà Plan. Some of these old neighbourhoods have kept all the distinctive character of the independent hamlets they once were.

Barri Gòtic – Following an intense restoration programme undertaken during the 1920s, the area containing the city's major historical buildings was renamed the Gothic quarter.

Ciutat Vella – The old city includes districts as varied as Santa Anna, La Mercè, Sant Pere and El Raval. The latter, which used to be known as the Barri Xino (Chinatown), now contains Barcelona's leading cultural centres and is a fine example of urban renovation.

Eixample – Eixample (el Ensanche) developed following the destruction of the city's medieval walls. The district personifies the bourgeois, elegant Barcelona of the end of the 19C, with its prestigious boutiques, smart avenues and some of the best examples of Modernist architecture, such as "La Pedrera" and "La Manzana de la Discordia".

Gràcia – This *barri*, situated at the end of the Passeig de Gràcia, is one of the city's most unique areas. Gràcia developed from its early agricultural origins into an urban area as a result of the influx of shopkeepers, artisans and factory workers. During the 19C, Gràcia was renowned for its Republican sympathies. Many

J. Malburet/MICHELIN

Passeig de Gràcia

associations took part in the workers' rebellions, including the 1870 uprising against "las quintas" (military conscription), during which the bell of Gràcia, in the tower in Rius y Taulet square, rang ceaselessly, and became a symbol for the rebellion.
Today, the neighbourhood hosts a number of popular events. On 15 August, the streets of Gràcia are bright with banners commemorating the feast of the Assumption, **La Mare de Déu d'Agost**, one of the most popular festivals of Barcelona. **Sant Medir**, another popular event, is celebrated by horsemen riding down **Gran de Gràcia** – the main business street – tossing sweets to the crowd.

La Ribera – With its narrow alleyways and Gothic architecture, this former fishermen's quarter still retains an unquestionable charm. Its main attractions are the Calle Montcada and the Iglesia de Santa María del Mar.

Sants – One of the city's main working class districts close to the railway station of the same name. It is a hodgepodge of industrial architecture, modest homes and a few late-19C shops

Les Corts – This district is located at the upper end of Diagonal and includes the **Ciudad Universitaria** and the **Camp Nou**, the Barcelona Football Club stadium (room for more than 120 000 fans). It is also home to the **Museu del Barça** *(☎ 93 496 36 08)*, with its display of all of the trophies awarded the Catalan team during its many years of existence.

Sarrià – Sarrià nestles at the foot of the Sierra de Collserola and has managed to retain its traditional, tranquil character. The neighbouring districts of **Pedralbes** and **Sant Gervasi de Cassoles**, at the foot of Tibidabo, have become a favourite hangout for the city's well-heeled inhabitants.

Horta-Guinardó – This *barri* at the foot of Collserola was first populated by peasants and then by factory workers. It is home to the **Laberinto de Horta** *(to the north)*, an 18C estate with a house built for the marquis d'Alfarràs, reflecting the eclectic tastes of the period. This park is adorned with statues of characters from mythology, niches and elements of Moorish architecture. There is a maze made of cypress hedges. The **Velódromo** is a venue for sporting events and major music events. The bars are especially popular in the summer.

Vila Olímpica – The Olympic Village was built to accommodate sportsmen and sportswomen participating in the 1992 games. Nowadays, it is a modern district with wide avenues, landscaped areas and direct access to some of Barcelona's restored beaches.

Poble Sec – On the slopes of Montjuïc, this is one of the oldest workers' districts of the city. Paralelo Street, once known for its cabarets and free-wheeling atmosphere, runs along one side of the neighbourhood for part of its length.

Barceloneta – A popular destination for its beaches, seafood restaurants and the pretty marina, this neighbourhood was created in 1714 to house the thousands left homeless after la Ribera was destroyed to make room for the enormous Ciutadella fortress.

Other neighbourhoods – the northern part of Barcelona has some very pleasant districts, including the tony **Vallvidriera** residential quarter, with a great view of the city. When the mountainside became accessible through roadways and public transportation, the Barcelona bourgeoisie rushed to outdo one another in country-home construction, and the hillsides are now dotted with outstanding examples of early 20C Modernist and Noucentist (a return to classical forms) architecture. Many of these former homes now house offices and schools. **Tibidabo**, the highest peak (512m), hosts a century-old amusement park and the popular Sagrat Cor church (an outstanding view). Nearby, **Sant Andreu** has preserved some

J. Malburet/MICHELIN

of its industrial heritage, while **Poblenou**, once known as the "Catalan Manchester", has many bars and concert halls.

El "Barça"? Aixó és més que un club

On October 22, 1899, an accountant of Swiss origin, Joan Camper, placed an advertisement in a daily paper seeking to find people to play football, a sport that was hardly known in Spain at the time. Thirty days later, in a gym in Barcelona, 12 young men founded the Fútbol Club Barcelona.

The members of the club, the city's largest, along with the RCD Espanyol, wear jerseys with blue and dark red stripes. The fans are known as "cules", in a reference to the first FCB stadium, whose design made it possible to contemplate the posteriors of 6 000 seated fans.

Since its inception, the "Barça" has counted some of the world's best trainers and players among its ranks, and entertained a longstanding rivalry with the Real Madrid.

The club's prestige is summed up in its informal slogan: *Aixó és més que un club* ("It's more than just a club").

J. Malburet/MICHELIN

Modernism

La Sagrada Familia

Imagination and technical revolution

Modernism developed between 1890 and 1920 alongside similar movements in other parts of Europe, such as Art Nouveau in both France and Great Britain and Jugendstil in Germany. Modernist architecture sprang from artistic exploration that combined new industrial materials with modern techniques, using decorative motifs like curve and counter-curve and asymmetrical shapes in stained glass, ceramics and metal.

The great architects

The most representative architects of the style were Antoni Gaudí, Domènech i Montaner, Puig i Cadafalch.

Antoni Gaudí (1852-1926) – Antoni Gaudí, born in Riudoms, studied architecture in Barcelona. His style was influenced first by Catalan neo-Gothic architecture with its emphasis on large areas of space (wide naves, the effect of airy spaciousness) and subsequently by the Islamic and Mudéjar styles. He also studied nature, observing plants and animals which inspired his shapes, colours and textures. He gave full rein to these images – liana-like curves, the rising and breaking of waves, rugged rocks and the serrations on leaves and flowers – when designing his fabulous buildings. Part of his great originality lay in his use of parabolic arches and spirals (as can be seen in the chimneys of Casa Milà). An intensely religious man, Gaudí drew upon a great many religious symbols for his buildings, especially for the Sagrada Familia (Church of the Holy Family) on which he worked for over 40 years. He spent his last years here, hidden away in a small room in the middle of the site, until his tragic death when he was run over by a tram.

Gaudí worked a great deal for the banker **Eusebi Güell**, his patron and admirer, who asked him to design his private houses. Gaudí's main works are the Sagrada Familia, Casa Batlló, La Pedrera (or Casa Milà), Casa Vicens, Palau Güell, Pavellons Güell and the Parc Güell.

Josep Puig i Cadafalch (1867-1956) – The mixture of regional and foreign architectural tradition in his work reflects the Plateresque and Flemish styles. His main works are the Casa de les Punxes, the Casa Macaya (1901) and the Casa Quadras (1904).

Lluis Domènech i Montaner (1850-1923) – He attained his highly decorative style through extensive use of mosaics, stained glass and glazed tiles. His main works include the Palau de la Música Catalana, Casa Lleó Morera, Castell dels Tres Dragons, Hospital de Sant Pau and Casa Montaner i Simó.

Imagination and technical revolution

alburet/MICHELIN

La Pedrera rooftop, A. Gaudí

Eixample★★

The word ***Eixample*** (in Catalan) or *Ensanche* (in Castilian) means enlargement or extension. Barcelona's Eixample was added to the city as a result of the **Cerdà Plan** in the 19C. A showcase for bourgeois homes in the late19C-early 20C, the district was a reflection of the economic and cultural prosperity of the times. In the 1950s, a literary movement known as la Renaixença, was born here; it is recognized as the predecessor of Modernism.

Eixample: modernisation of the city

The economic and demographic growth of the early 19C was too explosive to be contained within the old medieval walls of Barcelona. At various times, especially during periods of political instability, attempts had been made to tear them down, but they were always built up again. Finally, in 1851, the municipal authorities made an official request that the city cease to be fortified. Three years later, the walls came down.

In 1859 a call for bids went out for the design of an urban plan to encompass the new limits of the city. Municipal authorities selected a local architect, Antoni Rovira, to carry out the project, but the central government declared that the engineer **Ildefons Cerdà** (1815-1875) would do the job. Under the Rovira plan, the old town would have been the central hub for a streets extending outward like the spokes of a wheel. Cerdà, who had a clear vision of the future and pursued goals of social diversity as an antidote to the dehumanisation of industrial society, designed a network of streets 20m wide, parallel to the sea, bisected by large avenues. The plan called for blocks of housing with an open-air park or courtyard at the centre of each. Cerdà's framework was embraced, but city officials brushed aside his social goals and the number of parks and green spaces was reduced greatly, while the height of buildings increased. In the end, the Extension Plan resulted in creating a new Barcelona five times as big as the old city.

The Extension was carried out at one of the liveliest periods in the city's history. Industrial and economic development gave rise to a bourgeoisie that was committed to making Barcelona a great city. The creative expression of this dynamic was **Modernism**, in particular as expressed in the emblematic architecture of Eixample. Stroll through streets so carefully aligned and discover the beauty of Modernist architecture in the extravagantly decorated buildings as well as the small shops, pharmacies and bakeries. Note how the original use of materials such as iron, glass and ceramics makes each unique.

1 day, including museum visits

Plaça de Catalunya

The wide space left open by the demolition of the ramparts is the link between the old town and the Eixample. Built in 1927 by F. de P. Nebot, it has interesting sculptures by Llimona and de Gargallo, and a copy of *Deesa* by Josep Clarà, a masterpiece of noucentism. The Café Zurich is a classic spot at the top of the Rambla and a favourite meeting place.

Rambla de Catalunya*

This street runs through the Eixample and crosses the **Gran Vía de les Corts Catalanes**, before ending at Avinguda Diagonal, the two avenues that cross town.

The buildings in this busy part of town are alternately uninspired or modern. The mixture of older structures and striking iron-and-glass architecture makes a varied mosaic that is both authentic and surprising.

Fundació Antoni Tàpies**

Entrance on calle Aragó. ☎ 93 487 03 15. The foundation was created by the artist himself – who was born in Barcelona in 1923 – and set up in a former publishing house in the Modernist **Montaner i Simó*** building designed by Domènech i Montaner. The brick building is crowned by a large aerial sculp-

J. Pareto/TOURISME DE LA CATALOGNE

Fundació Antoni Tàpies

ture by Tàpies called ***Núvol i Cadira*** (cloud and chair), the emblem of the museum. It is a fitting example of the artist's symbolic universe.
The interior, a vast bare sober space where everything is painted in colours favoured by Tàpies (brown, beige, grey and ochre), is lit by skylights (a cupola and a pyramid) and sets off the artist's work remarkably well. The collection of over 300 paintings and sculptures tracing the development of Tàpies' work since 1948 is displayed on a rota basis.
Among the many works in the collection, those from the 1950-1960s, in the *serie matérica* (his "matter" works), are perhaps the most remarkable. After seeing the work of French artist Jean Dubuffet, Tàpies turned from Surrealism to Abstraction and began to question the basic medium of painting, paper. By the end of the 1960s, he was incorporating objects, unexpected materials such as straw, dirt, fluff, cardboard, graffiti, jute, clothing, cords, strings and rags to create dramatic effects.
The foundation is also a research centre and the wooden bookshelves that belonged to the publishing house that once operated in the building have been kept for a library. It holds an exhaustive collection on 20C artists in addition to archival material on Tàpies' work, and also significant resources on oriental arts and culture, which had a great influence on the artist.
Return to the Plaza de Catalunya and turn left to reach Passeig de Gràcia.

Passeig de Gràcia★★

Originally, this neighbourhood linked the old town to the village of Gràcia, but the Extension brought it within the confines of Barcelona and it became a wealthy residential area. Industrialists, politicians and glamorous women were the first to enjoy the wide avenue. The elegant wrought-iron **street lamps**★ were designed by Pere Falqués (1900), and the buildings are among the finest examples of Modernist architecture in Barcelona. Some of the master architects whose work stands here are Gaudí, Domènech i Montaner and Puig i Cadafalch.

"La Manzana de la Discordia"★★

(Apple of Discord)

Passeig de Gràcia between calles Consell de Cent and Aragó.
This block of houses owes its unusual name (a reference to the mythological task of Paris to award the golden apple to the most beautiful of the goddesses) to a word play on "manzana", which means both "apple" and "block of houses". One would be as hard-put as Paris to decide which of the three major Modernist architects created the most beautiful building.
Casa Lleó i Morera★ – At the corner of *Passeig de Gràcia and Consell de Cent.* This great stone edifice (1905) was built by Domènech i Montaner. The decoration, inspired by organic forms, is mostly concentrated around the bay windows and balustrades. The most interesting elements are the elaborate finials along the ridge of

the roof and the lantern-like crown at the top. The building is privately owned

Casa Amatller* – This building by Puig i Cadafalch has a lovely façade with floral frescoes and a stepped gable roof. Although not as extravagant as the works of Gaudi, the Catalan neo-Gothic windows – which the architect loved – and the wrought iron balcony railings and gates are exquisite.

The site is home to the **Amatller Institute**; on the ground floor the **Centro del Modernismo**, devoted to Art Nouveau in Barcelona, is open to the public for information *(for more information, see the Directory, Sightseeing)*.

Casa Batlló*** – ☎ *93 488 06 66*. This is one of Gaudí's greatest works, completed at the height of his creative powers (1904-1906). The **façade** is covered with ceramic and coloured glass. The roof is decorated with polychrome ceramics of brilliant colours, crowned by a tower; the design is typical of Gaudí's urban buildings. The unusual columns on the first floor earned the house the name "the Bone House". The exterior is astonishing, and the interior *(open to the public)* matches it in originality. Gaudí broke through many barriers to create a work of aesthetic coherence and unequalled beauty. The stairways, roof, patios, door and window frames, the use of light: each detail is part of a prodigious universe inspired directly by nature.

Near these emblematic buildings, in the "Manzana de la Discordia", stand other beautiful and significant works such as the **Casa Ramón Mulleras** (1911), designed by Enric Sagnier, and the **Casa Bonet** by Jaume Brossà.

M. Sagarra/TOURISME DE LA CATALOGNE

Casas Amatller and Batlló

Casa Milà (La Pedrera)★★★

☎ *902 40 09 73*. This is one of Gaudí's most famous works. Commonly known as La Pedrera ("the quarry"), the building was commissioned by the noble Milà family. Gaudí had planned a figure of the Virgin of the Rosary for the façade, full of Grace and protector of the Passeig, flanked by the archangels St. Gabriel and St. Michael, but they were never completed. There are two versions to explain this: the contractor affirmed that Mr. Milà did not like the sculpture created by Carles Mani and it was never cast in bronze; alternately, after the disturbances of July 26-20, 1909, the "Setmana Tràgica" (Tragic Week), when many churches in Barcelona were burned, Mr. and Mrs. Milà feared that their house could be confused with a convent or a church. Some reports say that Gaudí abandoned the project at that point, but if so, only a few chimneys remained unfinished. In 1986 La Pedrera was acquired by the Caixa de Catalunya (an important savings bank) with the intention of turning the building into a cultural and resource centre. Extensive restoration work was undertaken, lasting ten years. The **roof and the attic**, where one can see an exhibition on Gaudí and his works, are open to the public. Some flats are privately owned and the **main floor** is dedicated to the exhibition hall of the Centro Cultural Caixa Catalunya.

The building, the last secular work by the architect before he plunged into La Sagrada Familia, is an explosion of fantasy. It overshadows all the buildings around it on the passeig de Gràcia. The undulating design of the **façade**★★ recalls the sea, and the windows appear to be dug out of sand. The wrought-iron work on the balconies and windows is admirable.

Attic and roof★ – Gaudí constructed a series of catenary

La Pedrera

arches of various heights according to the widths of the bay. These arches sustain the walls of the exterior and interior façades of the attic at the sides, and the staggered roof above. The l'**Espai Gaudí** displays plans, models, photos and films on the life and work of the architect. The roof terrace is replete with strangely shaped chimneys and ventilators. The **views*** of Barcelona and the perspective on the building itself are well worth the visit.

Main Floor* (El Piso) – The exhibit area is divided into two sections: an exhibit on Barcelona of the period and the reconstitution of a bourgeois home from the early 20C, including the furnishings, the household appliances and other items of daily life commonly found in the homes of the well-heeled of that time.

La Pedrera was declared a World Heritage Site by UNESCO in 1984.

Avinguda Diagonal

This long avenue crosses the city, marking a diagonal track from East to West. On the upper end of the diagonal, you will find the **University campus** and **Camp Nou**, the stadium for the F.C. Barcelona. In this area, you can also visit the **Torres Trade***, on Gran Via de Carles III, a group of cylindrical towers with undulating bases, a fine symbol of the new trend in architecture in Barcelona, built in 1968 by **Josep A. Coderch**.

On plaça de Joan Carles I, turn right on Avinguda Diagonal.

As you walk along, notice the **Casa Quadras**, (no 373), an attractive Modernist building by Puig i Cadafalch (1904), with Catalan neo-Gothic influences.

Casa Terrades*

This edifice (1905) is better known as the **Casa de les Punxes** because of the points which crown the gables and towers of this curious mixture of Loire Valley chateau and mansion designed by Puig i Cadafalch. This is a pure expression of the Catalan neo-Gothic style.

La Sagrada Familia***

(Church of the Holy Family)

☏ *93 208 04 14.* This is Antoni Gaudí's best-known work. Dedicated to the Holy Family and to Saint Joseph, the patron saint of workers, the architect felt it to be an expiation of the materialistic modern world and an expression of the fraternity and solidarity among peoples.

Inspired by the Sacré-Cœur in Paris, Josep M. Bocabella, founder of a brotherhood devoted to Saint Joseph, conceived the idea of building a neo-Gothic church for his association. The work began in 1882, but was often interrupted by internal conflicts. In 1883, Gaudí joined the project and began by building the crypt. He then replaced the original plans with a much more ambitious blueprint. During the 40 years he spent on this work, he never ceased to complexify the symbolic character of the church – to a point that it became almost hermetic.

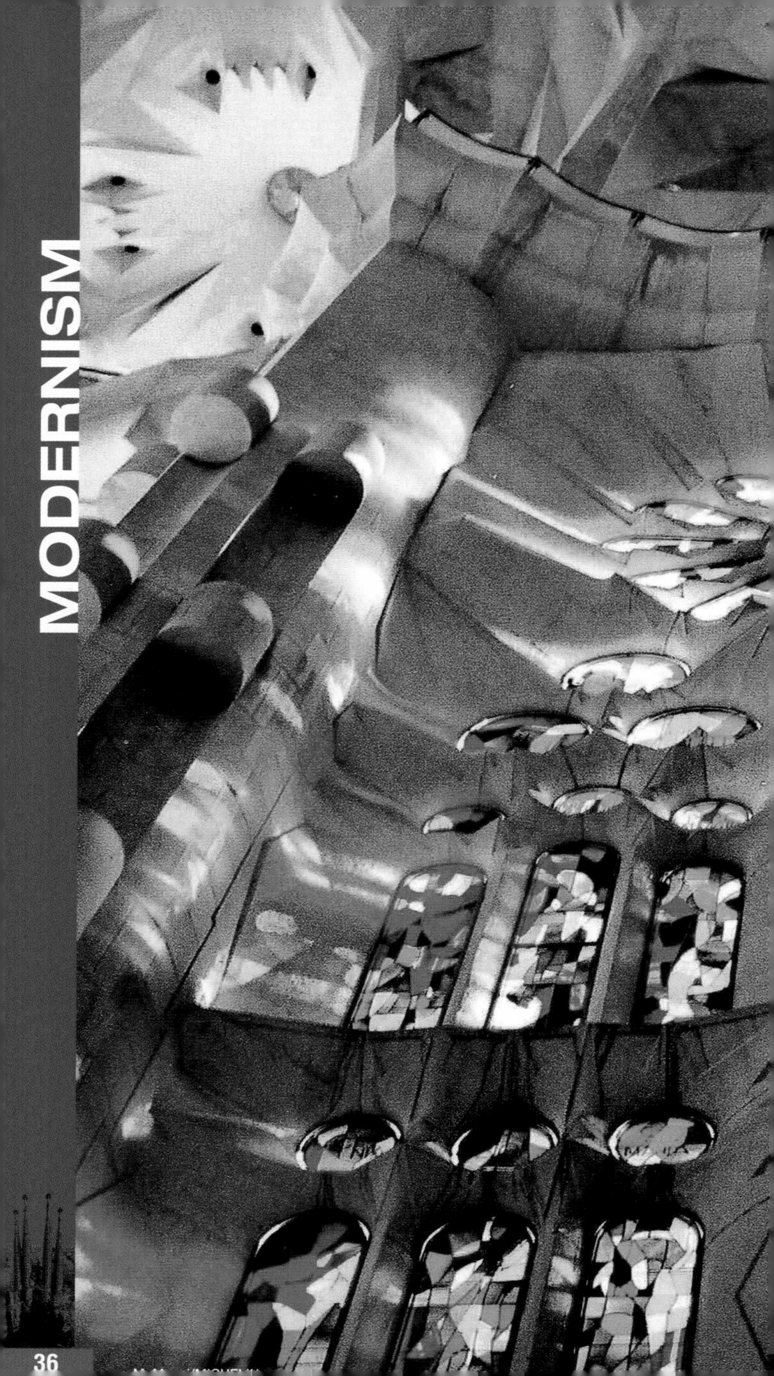

Eixample

Windows, Sagrada Familia

This revolutionary project of Gaudí's called for a ground plan in the form of a Latin cross with five naves and a transept with three naves. There were to be three façades: the Nativity, to the East on the right end of the transept, the Passion and Death on the opposite end, and Glory, on the façade facing South.

The four towers of each façade symbolised the 12 Apostles, while the great tower of the apse was a symbol of the Virgin Mary. Four large towers representing the Evangelists surrounded the spire over the transept crossing, a powerful symbol of Christ. The central nave was to resemble a forest of columns.

When Gaudí passed away, only the crypt, the apse and the Nativity façade had been finished. Despite lively polemic, it was finally determined that this great project would continue to go forward. Josep Maria Subirachs (1927) created the controversial sculptures on the Passion façade, the present-day entrance to the sanctuary.

Although the work going on inside creates a rather precarious situation, it is possible to climb the towers for an exceptional panoramic **view****.The image of la Sagrada Familia is most mysterious and disturbing at night, under illumination.

The Nativity façade** – Four towers 115m tall rise above the three doorways of this showy façade. To the left stands the Doorway of Hope, surmounted by the symbol of the Virgin Mary and scenes of the Holy Family. In the centre, the Doorway of Charity is decorated with a profusion of floral motifs; above the threshold you can see the family tree of Jesus and his monogram. The Doorway of Faith, with the symbol of Saint Joseph and sculptures showing the Visitation and the childhood of Jesus, is to the right.

Crypt – A stairway leads from the apse to the crypt. Gaudí's tomb is here, but it has also been fitted out to serve as a museum displaying plans, models and drawings of the different phases of construction and projects yet to be realized.

Hospital de Sant Pau*

Avinguda de Gaudí is where two of the most important Modernist architects meet: Lluís Domènech i Montaner and Antoni Gaudí. This large pedestrian walkway begins at the Nativity façade and continues as far as the entrance to Sant Pau Hospital, designed by Domènech i Montaner.

The red brick building (1902-1912) occupies more than 10 000sq m. To create this monumental work, the architect called on collaborators who included the prestigious sculptors **Pablo Gargallo** et **Eusebio Arnau**. The different pavilions are decorated with mosaics on the themes of mythology and the history of Cataluyna. The glazed ceramic tiles are in perfect harmony with the gardens where convalescents take the air.

Park Güell★★

☎ *93 413 24 00.* The park is the most famous of Gaudí's undertakings commissioned by Güell. Gaudí's extraordinary imagination is particularly evident here.

Visitors have the impression that they are entering an enchanted forest peopled with mushroom-shaped pavilions, a flight of steps climbed by a mosaic dragon, and avenues leading to an extravagant fantasy world. The artful combination of architecture and nature produces a curious effect, intermingling both rustic and fantastic elements. The **Chamber of the Columns**, in which an undulating mosaic roof covers a forest of sloping columns, and the remarkable **rolling bench**★★ are telling examples of the artist's fertile imagination.

A tour of the Park Güell ends with a visit to the **Casa-Museu Gaudí**★ *(☎ 93 219 38 11)*, located in the house where the famous architect once lived.

M. Sagarra/TOURISME DE LA CATALOGNE

Park Güell

Modernists buildings outside the Eixample

Palau de la Música Catalana**

☎ *93 295 72 00*. The building, in a neighbourhood of narrow streets, was expanded and transformed in 1989, and the surrounding buildings were recently restored in order to enhance the environment of the spectacular **exterior***. The lavish mosaic decoration and the sculptural work representing popular song – at the corner of the main entrance – were created bu Miquel Blay.

The interior, dominated by the large **inverted cupola**** of polychrome glass, is profusely and artistically decorated with sculpted groups and mosaic figurines.

To the left of the stage, a bust of **Josep Anselm Clavé** (1824-1874), a musician who founded many popular choral groups, symbolises Catalan music. To the right, in memory of the strong influence of Wagner's music on musical circles in Barcelona, is an

M. Sagarra/TOURISME DE LA CATALOGNE

Palau de la Música Catalana, interior detail

extraordinary **Valkyrie** next to a bust of Beethoven, an allusion to international music. These dynamic sculptures by Gargallo are the counterpoint to the unusual **mosiac silhouettes** and the **bust in relief**, the fruit of the creative imagination of Eusebi Arnau, placed at the back of the stage. A wealth of surprising details fill this space, where the showy atmosphere is restrained by the well-worn seats, the understated mosaics and the play of coloured light from the windows.

Palau Güell**

☎ *93 317 39 74*. This unique building, the residence of the Güell family, which counted ten children, was built by Gaudí from 1886-1890.

On the **façade***, in white stone, there are Catalan symbols such as the dragon and the "four bars", embellished with imaginary motifs and the initials of **Eusebi Güell**. The stone and iron building is fronted with two entrances forming parabolic arches, large enough for horse-drawn carts to enter, embellished with magnificent wrought-iron gates flanked by two serpents. The building clearly reflects the personal ideas of the architect and his conception of space. The innovative use of materials (notice the floor in the hall, which imitates brick tiles), the importance of light as an element to unify space, wooden doors and ceilings (some uncommonly beautiful) are keys elements in this magnificent townhouse designed entirely by an architect of genius.

The interior is dominated by a three-storey **Reception Room** topped with a huge parabolic dome which lets in light via star-shaped windows, for a celestial effect.

The crowning glory of Palau Güell is the roof, Gaudí's "fifth façade" dotted with 20 different mosaic-covered sculptures which turn the chimneys, ventilation covers, and stairwells into works of art.

Pabellones Güell*

☎ *93 204 52 50*. These former stables were renovated by Gaudí; note the remarkable **wrought-iron gate** decorated with a dragon.

J. Malburet/MICHELIN

Exploring the city

Plaça de la Boqueria, la Rambla

Barri Gòtic★★

The "Gothic" district is so-called because of the buildings dating from the 13, 14 and 15C. In fact, it is much older, as Roman ruins are also found there. Parts of the 4C wall surrounding the city are still visible in some places. During the 19C, the most damaged monuments were carefully restored, and today the neighbourhood is quite beautiful.
The pedestrian street Portal de l'Ëngel, that goes from the Plaça de Catalunya into the Barri Gòtic, Portaferissa and other neighbouring streets that link the Barri to La Rambla are among the busiest shopping streets.
Allow 2h including the visit of the Cathedral.

Plaça Nova

This is the heart of the Gothic quarter. The Romans built a rectangular site with walls 9m/30ft high and attendant watch-towers of which the two that guarded the West Gate remain to this day. In the Middle Ages, when the town expanded beyond the walls, the gateway was converted into a house. On August 16th, the Feast of Saint Roc is celebrated with dancing the Sardana in the streets. On one side, the square is bordered by the Baroque façade of the **Palau del Bisbe** (bishops' palace). Opposite the cathedral, the **Collegi d'Arquitectes** (College of Architects) stands out as an architectural surprise among the old buildings. Its modern façade has a decorative band of cement engraved by Picasso.

Pla de la Seu

The Avinguda de la Catedral, which joins Plaça Nova to Via Laietana, is a large promenade popular with roller-skaters that leads to the impressive Cathedral steps rising up from Pla de la Seu. This square, built in 1421, is famous for the festival held here every December 8th, the **Fira de Santa Llúcia**, a popular fair where figures for Christmas crèches are the main attraction.
Around the square stand the houses la Pia Almoina, la Canonja and l'Ardiaca.

Casa de la Canonja

Once the residence of the canons of the Cathedral (1546), the building has unusual details sculpted on the façade and inside. To the right of it stands la **Pia Almoina**, a charitable institute founded in 1009 to succour the poor of the city. Both buildings have been totally renovated and today house the **Museum of the Dioceses of Barcelona,** where paintings, sculptures, gold and silverwork and vestments are on display. Temporary exhibits are also held here. (*Entrance on Avinguda de la Catedral, ☏ 93 315 22 13*).

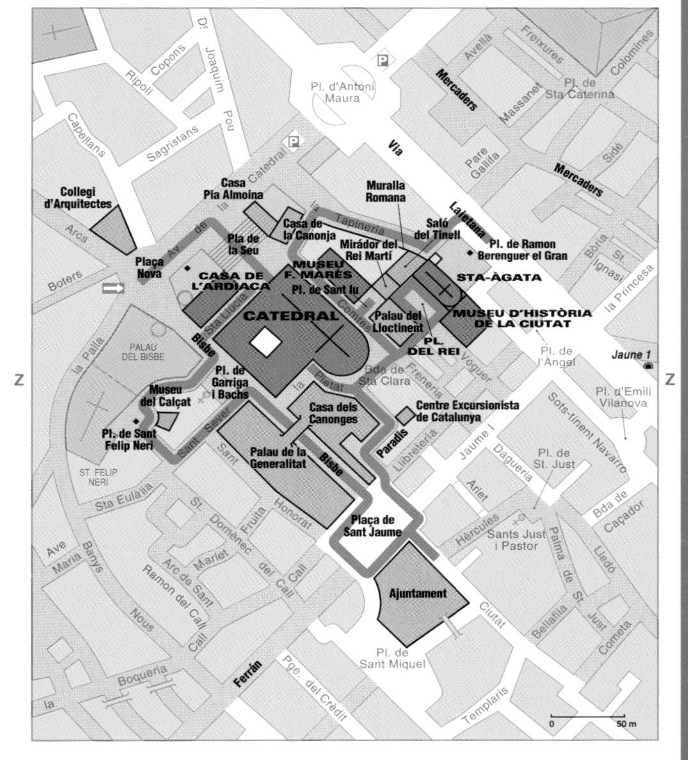

Catedral★

☎ *93 315 15 54 or 93 315 22 13*. The Cathedral, known as La Seu, is officially named Catedral de la Santa Creu i Santa Eulalia, after Barcelona's patron saint Eulalia. By 343 A.D., under Roman occupation, a basilica was built at the site of the current Cathedral. In 985 it was largely destroyed by the Moors, led by Al-Mansur. It was replaced by a Romanesque cathedral, built between 1046 and 1058. A chapel, the Capella de Santa Llúcia, was added between 1257 and 1268. It was later incorporated in the cloister next to the cathedral. In 1298, construction of the Gothic catedral started under King Jaume II, known as 'the Just'. Most of the Romanesque edifice was demolished at that time, except for the Santa Llúcia chapel. Due to civil wars and the Black Death that hit the city several times, the construction only progressed slowly. It took until 1460 before the main building was completed.

The **main façade** was finished much later, in 1889 and the last part, the central spire, was completed in 1913.

The plans for the façade, the spire, the gables and the pinnacles were based on the original design from 1408 by the French architect Charles Galters.

Interior★ – The three naves are in the pure Catalan neo-Gothic style. The naves soar upward thanks to the lightness of the slim pillars and the steady, indirect lighting provided by the lantern, located above the entrance, rather than at the transept crossing, as is usually the case. To the right of the main entrance is the **Chapel of the Holy Eucharist** (Capella del Santíssim), a former chapter house with an octagonal, vaulted ceiling. Begun in 1400, it was rebuilt in the 17C to receive the tomb of Saint Olegarius. The crucifix in this chapel, known as the Christ of Lepanto (15C), is said to have been on the prow of the galley commanded by Don Juan de Austria during the battle of Lepanto (1571).

In the next chapel **(1)**, devoted to Saints Cosme and Damien, there is an admirable **Gothic altar screen** by Bernat Martorell. The fifth chapel **(2)** contains the tomb of **Raimundo de Peñafort** (14C), a Dominican, and one of the most venerated local saints.

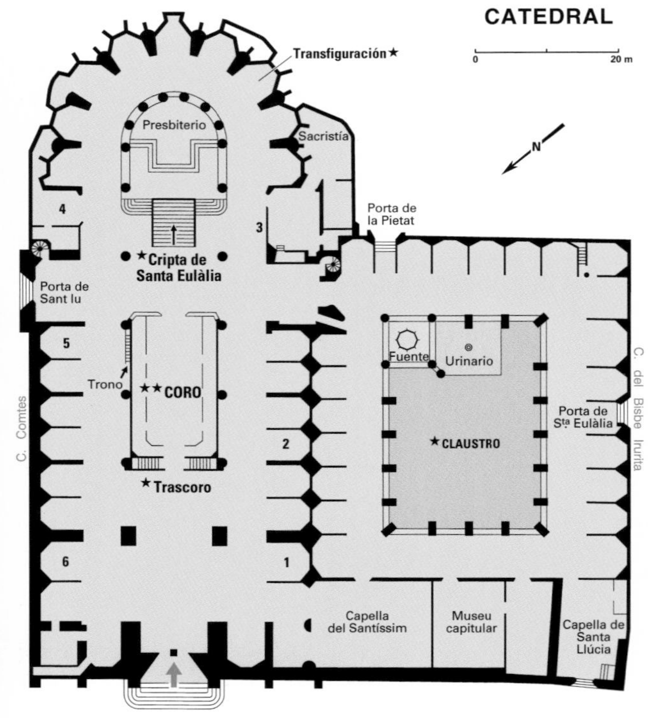

The Cathedral roof

Lift to go up. Metal walkways, dominated by the imposing silhouettes of the towers and the lantern of the Cathedral provides a unique and splendid **view**★★ over Barcelona, from the narrow streets of the old town to the grid of Eixample and the Montjuïc mountains, and all the way to the sea shore on one side and the sierra de Collserola on the other. Rising tall out of the urban landscape are the octagonal towers of Santa Maria del Pi, the towers of la Sagrada Familia and the Olympic Villages.

Adjacent to the Cathedral is a 14C cloister. There are always 13 geese in its central courtyard. Each goose represents one year in the life of the martyr Santa Eulalia, tortured to death in the 4C by the Romans for her religion.

East End – Under the main altar and the transept crossing lies the **crypt of Saint Eulalia**, covered by a low, ribbed, vault. There are very interesting sculptural details on the steps leading to the chapel where the saint's sarcophagus rests. It is in alabaster, made by Tuscan artists in the 14C. To the right of the presbyterium (area in front of the altar), against a wall, are the **tombs** of the founders of the Romanesque cathedral **(3)**: Ramon Berenguer the Elder and his wife Almodis.

The side chapels have Gothic and Baroque altar screens, including a masterpiece, The **Transfiguration**★, by Bernat Martorell, one of the greatest works of Catalan painting from the past.

In the eastern arm of the transept, above the door of Sant Iu, is the monumental organs.

Choir★★ – As in most Spanish cathedrals and collegiate churches, the choir *(coro)* is enclosed by finely sculpted Gothic walls. There are two rows of polychrome stalls: the upper level, with richly ornamented backrests surmounted by carved finials, was created around the end of the 14C. The lower row dates from the mid-15C.

In 1519, during a meeting of the Order of the Golden Fleece, the backrests were decorated with the coat of arms of each knight. Jean de Bourgogne created one of the most extraordinary collections of heraldic symbols in all of Europe. Note the delicacy and humour of the misericordes of the stalls.

You reach the Bishop's throne *(trona)* by a stone stairway embellished with two wrought iron works: a balustrade with fleurs de lis and a gate. The octagonal throne is made of wood, carved with many decorative figures.

The **Trascora** (the back side of the choir) was erected in the 16C; it is made of white marble and was designed by Bartolomé Ordóñez – who probably worked on the stalls as well –, and was completed by Pierre Villar after Ordóñez' death.

Walk down the left side aisle and you will pass in front of the chapel of the Virgin of Montserrat **(5)**, the patron of Cataluyna, known here as "la Moreneta". Veneration of this figure began around the mountain of the same name,

J. Malburet/MICHELIN

Detail of the choir

where a monastery was created in the early 4C. Farther down, you can admire the superb altar screen of Saint Mark **(6)**, patron saint of cobblers.
Cloisters* – This is one of the most peaceful places in town. Four galleries with ogee vaulting surround a patio where palm trees, magnolia, medlar and orange trees grow around a fountain dedicated to Sant Jordi (Saint George), patron of Cataluyna and Aragon. The 15C urinal adds a humble touch to this otherwise celestial oasis. The chapels in the galleries are adorned with wrought-iron work (admire the 14C floral motifs) and some of the chapels still have unusual old altar screens. In the north wall, Mossén Borrá, jester to King Alphonse V, is buried.
Museu capitular – Two gorgeous rooms are set aside for the Cathedral Museum. There are a few 15C paintings, including *La Pietàt* by Bartolomé Bermejo, where you will find an echo of the sculpture on the Pietà Doorway. Also worth note are the late medieval tomb of the archdeacon Luis Desplà and Saint Eulalia's missal, embellished with fine miniatures.
Capella de Santa Llúcia – This chapel is worth special attention, for it is all that remains of the Romanesque cathedral. It was built in 1268 and is dedicated to Santa Llúcia, the patron saint of eyesight and intelligence, and well-loved in Barcelona.
Leave the Cathedral by the Santa Llùcia Doorway, located across from the Archdeacons' house.

Casa de l'Ardiaca*

Built in the 12C, on the Roman wall, the Archdeacons' house was enlarged around the 15C by Archdeacon Luis Desplà, to lend greater dignity to his office.
The house has three façades. The main one faces the Santa Llùcia Chapel, the second is turned to Carrer del Bisbe Irurita and the third to Pla de la Seu. This building mixes Gothic and Renaissance decorative elements. Admire the small **inner courtyard***, a peaceful haven decorated with a border of glazed tile. Although it was added in 1920, the border fits in harmoniously. The upper floor is home to the **Arxiu Històric de la Ciutat** (Municipal Historical Archives).

Plaça Sant Felip Neri

The Renaissance houses surrounding this small square were moved here when via Laietana was being built, to make room for the new street. The square is home to the unusual **Museu del Calçat**, a shoe museum whose exhibits include Columbus' shoes.
Take Sant Felip Neri and return to Carrer del Bisbe Irurita by way of Sant Sever.

Carrer del Bisbe

After the bishops' palace, you will see the little **Plaça Garriga i Bachs**. Facing it, the Santa Eulàlia Doorway opens to the cloisters. The monument on one side, dedicated to the citizens of Barcelona who died during the

J. Malburet/MICHELIN

Palau de la Generalitat

S. Ollivier/MICHELIN

Covered gallery, Carrer del B

Napoleonic occupation, is the work of **Josep Llimona** (1864-1934). The right of the street is bordered by the **Casa dels Canonges** (Canons' Residence), now the residence of the President of the Generalitat. A Catalan neo-Gothic covered gallery (1929), over a star-vaulted arch, spans the street to link the two buildings.

Plaça Sant Jaume

This square was the main crossroads of the Roman town: the cardo and the decumanous. At that time, it was the also the site of the agora. Today, two buildings symbolising 14C Barcelona stand here: the Town Hall and the Palau de la Generalitat.

Palau de la Generalitat (Provincial Council) – ☏ *93 402 46 16*. La Generalitat appeared in the 14C as a Commission of the Catalan Parliament, made of up two representatives of the three estates (the clergy, the nobility, the urban bourgeoisie). Its main function was to collect taxes.

The palace is a great building of three storeys, built in the early 15C in the Gothic style and later remodelled. The façade on Plaça Sant Jaume, built around 1600 by Pere Blay, the most important Catalan architect of the period, it is a fine example of Renaissance architecture.

Ajuntament (Town Hall) – ☏ *93 402 73 00*. The Town Hall stands across from the Palau de la Generalitat. It was built in the last third of the 14C, but its main façade, in neo-Classical style, was added on later (19C). The **Gothic façade** (circa 1400) facing rue de la Ciutat is the oldest and most interesting. On the doorway, you can see a stone carving of Saint Raphael and the coats-of-arms of the city and the king.

The "Call" of Barcelona

It was the neighbourhood of one of the most prosperous Jewish communities in the Mediterranean region. Behind the Palau de la Generalitat, the names of the streets recall the past (Carrer del Call, de Sant Doménech del Call, Baixada de Santa Eulàlia, Carrer dels Banys Nous). Jewish presence in Barcelona is one of the best documented in Spain. For example, it is known that a significant number of the Jews in the district were craftsmen, financiers, moneychangers and booksellers. Many were wealthy property owners, not only in the district but also in the area around the community cemetery, on Mount Montjuïc. The community was well-integrated and business exchanges with the Christian community were common. At the end of Calle Marlet, there is a copy of a fragment of an inscription in Hebrew – the original is in the Museu d'Història de la Ciutat. It indicates that a charitable centre occupied the site and is one of the few vestiges of the old Jewish quarter.

The inside of the building has changed almost entirely since its origins. 16-17C rooms were mostly destroyed for remodelling. Yet the **Saló de Centa** is worth seeing. It was a meeting room for the Consell des Cent, or general assembly, the forerunner of the municipal council. Although often renovated, it still has a remarkably rich décor.

Carrer del Paradís

This street owes its name to the garden that once flourished here. At **no 10**, a Gothic building now serves as the offices of the **Centre Excursionista de Catalunya**, an alpinists' club founded in 1876. On this same spot, in honour of Augustus, the city's greatest temple once rose. The ruins can be seen by crossing the patio. Four Corinthian columns, spectacular vestiges of the city's Roman heritage, have been entirely preserved.

Carrer del Paradis leads to Carrer de la Pietat, which circles around part of the east end of the Cathedral and is bordered on the other side by the Gothic façades of the Caonons' houses. The door that leads to the cloisters, the Pietà Doorway is surmounted by a 16C wooden *Pietà*.

Return to Baixada de Santa Clara.

Plaça del Rei**

On this splendid square stand some of the important medieval buildings of the city: the Palau Reial Major (at the back), the Capilla de Santa Àgata (on the right) and the Palau del Lloctinent. In the right-hand corner is the Casa Clariana-Padellàs, which houses the **Museu d'Història de la Ciutat**** *(see description under Museums; the visit of the museum includes the the interior of the Palau Reial Major, from the Capilla de Santa Àgueda to the Saló del Tinell)*, housed in a fine 15C Gothic mansion that was moved here stone by stone while the via Laietana was being built in 1931.

Palau Reial Major – Initially built in the 11C and 12C, the palace was gradually enlarged over the years until it acquired its present appearance in the 14C. It used to be the official residence of the counts of Barcelona and subsequently that of the kings of Aragón. The **façade**

EXPLORING THE CITY

J. Malburet/MICHELIN

Plaça del Rei

features huge buttresses linked together by arches. At the back of these arches lies the original Romanesque façade with its trilobate windows and Gothic rose windows. A side staircase leads to the **Mirador del Rei Martí**, a five-storey tower.

Capilla de Santa Águeda** – This 14C palatine chapel has a single nave is covered by intricate polychrome woodwork panelling. It was consecrated to Saint Agatha in the 17C.

Palau del Lloctinent – This palace was built between 1549 and 1557 to be used as a residence for "lieutenants" of the king, otherwise known as the Viceroys of Cataluyna, after Spanish unification. The three façades, one on the la Plaça del Rei, another on la baixada de Santa Clara and the third on Carrer dels Comtes are austere. The late Gothic style predominates with Renaissance elements, as was typical in 16C architecture.

The main entrance on Carrer dels Comtes leads to a beautiful Italianate **patio** with wide archways on the ground floor. On the upper floor, the a Tuscan-style gallery and an elegant stairway.

Plaça de Sant Iu

This very small square is one of the busiest places in the Barri Gòtic; something is always happening, be it a mime show or musicians livening up the streets. From here, you can visit the Cathedral or the **Museu Frederic Marès** *(see "Other museums and sights of interest")*, which has been in an outbuilding of the Palau Reial since 1948.

Continue along Carrer dels Comtes then turn onto Carrer de la Tapineria.

Plaça de Ramon Berenguer el Gran

This is one of the images most symbolic of old Barcelona. Behind the bronze equestrian statue of Ramon Berenguer III, the work of sculptor Josep Llimona, there is a landscaped park surrounded by cypress trees. At the bottom of the garden, you can see a good section of the Roman wall where it leads to calles de la Tapineria and des Murallas Velles. 18m high with two storeys and semi-circular windows, three of the seven original towers have been thoroughly preserved. At the foot of the old walls you can see a few ancient Roman *cupas*, blocks of stone or marble bearing inscriptions.

In the 13C, the three towers were linked by vaults so that another floor could be built above the royal palace.

La Rambla★★

Better known as **"Las Ramblas"**, because it is sectioned off in several blocks with different names, La Rambla stretches from Plaça de Catalunya to the Christopher Columbus monument on Plaça Portal de la Pau. This colourful and lively thoroughfare was originally a rushing stream that marked the western limits of the city. Improved between the 15-17C, in the 19C it became the famous promenade that we know today.

The upper section, closest to Plaça de Catalunya, is the **Rambla de Canaletes**, for the fountain of the same

J. Malburet/MICHELIN

name that is found there. Tradition has it that visitors who drink from the fountain are sure to return to Barcelona. This pedestrian section of las Ramblas is usually filled with the sound of animated conversations on every subject – football and politics seeming to be the most contentious.
The following section, La **Rambla dels Estudis**, is named for Barcelona's first university – El Estudio General – which once stood on the spot. It is also known as Rambla dels Ocells (birds) because many sparrows gather in the trees there and you find kiosks selling small animals, mostly (obviously) birds. There are also chickens, parrots, turtles, hamsters and fish for sale, though.

Turn left on Portaferrissa, a busy shopping street.

Palau Moja

This late Baroque building from the end of the 18C was home to the great poet **Jacint Verdaguer** (1845-1902); the influences of French neo-Classicism can be seen in the pure lines. The frescoes in the great hall are remarkable. Since its restoration in 1982, it has become the headquarters for the **Direccio General del Cultural patrimony, Generalitat de Catalunya** (General Cultural Heritage Directorate) And temporary exhibits are held there.

Return to La Rambla and cross to the other side.

Iglesia de Betlem

The first public Christmas cribs were organised in this Baroque-style church (17-18C), which was part of a Jesuit monastery. Only the monumental Baroque façade on Carrer del Carme was saved after a fire destroyed the interior in 1936. The twisted columns are remarkable.

Follow Carrer del Carme.

Hospital de la Santa Creu

This hospital centre is one of the most important initiatives undertaken during the reign of Martin I. Before its foundation (1401), the hospitals in different parts of the city were managed by the Church and religious orders. With the construction of this hospital ("Holy Cross"), hospital services were centralised and the city also gained a significant architectural ensemble.

Carrer del Carme leads to the narrow patio that provides access to the three monumental buildings of the old hospital. On the right, stands the stone façade of the **Convalescence House**, which appears quite plain, but conceals within a vestibule of exuberant decoration: polychrome mosaic plinths and a two-storey patio with Tuscan-style columns. It is currently the headquarters of the Institute for Catalonia Studies.

On the left, the façade used to belong to the Surgical College, and now fronts the medical school.

At the far end of the courtyard, the central patio is currently known as the Rubio y Lluch gardens.

Central patio★ – The vastness of this rectangular Gothic patio with its landscaping is breathtaking. Two central stairways lead to the immense rooms on the upper floors where patients were cared for, today home of the Library of Catluyna, a private library founded in 1914. The Massana Academy of Fine Arts is next door.

Go back to La Rambla and the Betlem church.

La **Rambla de les Flors**, or Rambla de Sant Josep, is an explosion of colours. Quintessence of the city, this narrow promenade with lime trees growing along either side (brought here from Gerona at the end of the 19C) is lined with flower shops. The famous Catalan painter **Ramón Casas** (1866-1932), the first regional painter to use Impressionist techniques, often painted the bright avenue and even married a florist who worked there.

Palau de la Virreina*

At the end of the 18C, Manuel Amat, a nobleman who had been Viceroy of Peru, returned to Barcelona with a great fortune. To show off his wealth, he built this luxurious palace, a mixture of Baroque and Rococo styles. It hosts major temporary exhibitions.

At the beginning of La **Rambla del Centre** (also **Carrerd dels Caputxins)**, you can see the paving designed by Joan Miró for la **Pla de la Boqueria**, a small esplanade facing the entrance to the **Mercat de Sant Josep** – or de la Boqueria –, a traditional covered market. It is the city's best market, with an enticing array of colours and fragrances that will sweep you off your feet.

In times past, many religious buildings stood along this section, but revolutions and fires got the better of them and now there is a procession of cafés, hotels and souvenir stands drawing "pilgrims" in the summertime.

Turn left on Cardenal Casañas.

Iglesia de Santa Maria del Pi*

☎ *93 318 47 43.*

This large 14C Basilica was built with many chapels and many public and private ceremonies were celebrated there over the centuries. Many corporations met in the neighbourhood and the various brotherhoods considered the church as their place of worship. Santa Maria del Pi stands

J. Malburet/MICHELIN

House decorated with frescoes, Plaça del Pi

on the pleasant little **Plaça del Pi.** The building at **no 1** is embellished with sgraffiti; it was the meeting house of the brotherhood of the Very Holy Blood, whose members carried out a very particular act of penitence: they accompanied condemned prisoners to the scaffold.
The main façade of the church faces the square and is remarkable for the big rose window, flanked by two unfinished towers.
The interior is typical of Catalan Gothic churches (a single nave and side chapels). The simplicity of the decoration brings out the beauty of the architecture and the volume of the central nave lends a solemn atmosphere.

Plaça de Sant Josep Oriol*

In front of the side façade of Santa Maria del Pi, a busy square is home to a monument erected in memory of the playwright **Guimerà** (1845-1924). It is a favourite meeting place for both tourists and the art crowd; many painters, musicians and poets meet up in the cafés of this picturesque little corner of town.
Go back to La Rambla.

Gran Teatre del Liceu

☎ 93 485 99 14. The theatre was completely rebuilt after the fire of 1994.
The theatre opened its doors in the mid-19C, thanks to the cultural association Liceu Filhàrmonico-Dramàtic Barcelonès, financed by the bourgeoisie of Barcelona. The first building, the work of J. O. Mestres and M. Garriga i Roca, was built on the site of the former convent of the Trinitaires, was inaugurated in 1847. In 1861 a fire devastated it, but it was rebuilt in one year.
A popular meeting place for the bourgeoning industrial and financial bourgeoisie, the Liceu became a favourite target of anarchist groups, who carried out a serious attack there in 1893.
Since the early 20C, the theatre has been the scene of world premiers for some great contemporary composers. Renowned singers have performed here and the ballet season is very prestigious.
Turn right on Nou de La Rambla.

Palau Güell**

This large pedestrian square was created between 1840 and 1850 on the site of a former Capuchin monastery, according to plans drawn by

BARCELONA, LAND OF OPERA

The Liceu has provided the people of Barcelona with the opportunity to develop a taste for opera. Some of the great lyric performances of all time have taken place here. Among the talented artists who have graced the stage of the Liceu: soprano **Montserrat Caballé**, appreciated for the power of her voice and her distinguished interpretation of *Lucrecia Borgia*; **José Carreras**, the admirable tenor who has excelled in works by Verdi ; **Victoria de los Ángeles** (1923-2005), whose fine soprano voice is pure and smooth; **Jaume Aragall**, a tenor specialised in the Italian repertory.

Francesc D. Molina, who found inspiration in both French boulevards and Castilian squares.

The former residence of the Güell family (1886-1890) is a unique building designed by Gaudí in 1889. Note the parabolic arches at the **entrance*** and the extravagant wrought-iron work so typical of the Modernist movement. *(See Modernism: Modernist buildings around the Eixample.)*

Return to La Rambla and cross over.

Plaça Reial**

This large pedestrian square was created between 1840 and 1850 on the site of the former Capuchin monastery, according to plans drawn up by Francesc D. Molina, who was inspired both by French boulevards and Castilian squares.

The harmony of the architecture is achieved by handsome, high arcaded buildings, embellished with medallions honouring navigators and explorers. Two fanciful street lights designed by the young Gaudí and a stand of palm trees complete the ensemble.

At night the square is popular for the *cervecerías* (beer bars) under the arcades and on Sunday there is a stamp and coin market.

Don't forget to have a look in the **passeig Bacardí**, and iron and glass gallery that is reminiscent of Paris.

The square is linked by a passage to the **Carrer de Ferran**, a long shopping street that leads to Sant Jaume square, and on the other side to **Carrer dels Escudellers**, where the ambience of the Barri Chino is felt. Between these two streets, as you approach Sant Jaume square, you can see **Carrer d'Avinyó**, whose bordellos are said to have inspired Picasso to paint *Les demoiselles d'Avignon* (1907).

Return to La Rambla.

The **Pla del Teatre** is an esplanade where the old Principal theatre stands, alongside a monument to the satiric dramatist Frederic Soler, better known as **"Pitarra"**. Caricaturists, painters and card readers have taken over the square, lending it a lively, if somewhat unreal ambience.

La **Rambla de Santa Mònica** is the intersection of La Rambla and the sea. Along this wide promenade, you can see the **Palau Marc**, a fine neo-Classic building with a covered interior patio, housing offices of the Direcció General de Patrimoni Cultural, and the former **Santa Mònica Convent**, now the Centre d'Art Santa Mònica, where temporary exhibits are shown. *(☎ 93 316 28 10/27 27)*.

Behind the Palau Marc is the **Wax Museum** *(see "Other museums and sights of interest")*.

Columbus Memorial

☎ *93 302 52 24*. On **Plaça Portal de la Pau**, just before the shipyards *(see below)*, rises the Christopher Columbus Monument. Built in 1886 by Gaietà Buïgas, it commemo-

J. Malburet/MICHELIN

rates the reception held by the Catholic kings in honour of the navigator from Genoa after his first voyage to America. A great cast iron column set on a stone base bears the statue of the explorer. At the time of its construction, the statue represented a great symbol of progress by its use of iron. Today, it is emblematic of Barcelona, more for its prestige than its beauty. From the top of the narrow tower, 52m high *(not recommended for those who suffer fear of heights or claustrophobia)*, visitors can enjoy a **panoramic view**★ of the city.

Drassanes (Shipyards)★★

The **rope works** here are among the best examples of non-religious Gothic architecture in Catalunya. Ten sections – seven from the 14C and three beside La Rambla from the 17C – remain from the former shipyards; they are covered by a long timber roof supported by a row of sturdy arches carved in stone. They are the largest surviving medieval shipyards in the world

During the reign of Pedro III el Grande (1240-1285), a building went up with a fortified patio surrounded by porches

Plaça Reial

and defensive towers on the corners. Pedro IV. El Ceremonioso (1336-1387) expanded the porches on the east and west ends and transformed them into vaulted rooms made up of eight parallel naves where it was possible to work on 30 galleys at a time. Around the end of the 16C; the workshops became the property of the Generalitat. Eight more naves, each more than 100m long, were added. With the discovery of the "New World", the Atlantic horizon became more important than the shores of the Mediterranean, and shipbuilding in Barcelona fell into decline as a consequence. The shipyards were broken apart and transformed into artillery quarters. In 1936, military authorities transferred the property to the city. The oldest buildings standing are now home to the **Museu Maritim** (maritime museum) *(see "Other museums and sights of interest")*.

The waterfront★

The waterfront runs from the foot of the Montjuïc Mountain to the mouth of the Besòs river. The whole district was completely redesigned and upgraded for the 1992 Olympic Games. Ironically, Barcelona, which has always turned its back to the sea, is now regarded as a coastal city.

The N° 14 bus line runs along the waterfront as far as the Olympic Village.

The renovation of the waterfront district in Barcelona began with the urban project of **Moll de Bosch i Alsina**, also known as **Moll de la Fusta** (Wood Wharf), an attractive raised promenade lined with palm trees.

J. Malburet/MICHELIN

Used until the mid-20C to store wood before shipment, this wharf has become one of the liveliest areas of town. Alongside the contemporary sculptures by artists such as Robert Krier and Roy Lichtenstein, ships are docked and yachts bob serenely in the marina, the Real Club Nautico and the Real Club Maritima.

Port Vell*

The **old port** is now devoted to leisure and recreation. A wooden bridge, La Rambla **de Mar**, leads to the Moll d'Espanya, which you can follow to reach the **Aquarium** *(see "Other musems and sights of interest")* and the **Maremagnum**, a big mall with restaurants, cafés, multiplex cinemas, bars, discotheques and the **IMAX** *(☎ 93 225 11 11)*, with its spectacular 180°screen and a programme of documentaries and concert films.

Port Vell

Take the Promenade de Colón, then turn left on Carrer d'en Serra.

Basílica de la Mercè*

☎ *93 310 51 51.* The present-day Basilica, dedicated to the patron saint of Barcelona, dates from 1760. Despite the damages suffered during the Civil War, both façades have been perfectly preserved. The main façade, on Plaça de la Mercè, is the only example in Barcelona of a curved Baroque façade. In Carrere Ample, the other facade is in Renaissance style. It was moved here from a neighbouring church in 1870.

The cupola, an eclectic 19C addition, is surmounted by a monumental statue of the Virgin of la Mercè, visible from many different places in the city.

The interior, with a single nave and side chapels, is richly decorated with marble and large windows with intricate blinds. The lovely Gothic **statue*** of the **Virgin de la Mercè**, by Pere Moragues (1361), is especially interesting.

Continue along Passeig Colom as far as Vía Laietana.

Vía Laietana

This major thouroughfare, which crosses the old town and goes to the port, was opened in the first decade of the 20C, necessitating the demolition or removal of many large buildings.

Follow along Passeig d'Isabel II.

La Llotja*

☎ *908 44 84 48.* Originally, the **Exchange Market** was held in the open air; goods arriving from the port were traded here. As Barcelona grew in commercial importance, it became necessary to provide better accommodation for traders, and, at the end of the 14C, merchants undertook the construction of a vast building that was to become the Consolat de Mar. The current building was put up in the late 18C, in neo-Classical style.

The main façade on Carrer de Consolat de Mar, as well as the side façades, were realised according to French models of monumental architecture. The building now serves as headquarters for the Chamber of Commerce and Industry.

All that remains of the medieval edifice in the great **Gothic hall****, whose lofty proportions are matched only by the "Loggia" in Florence. The three naves are separated by triple round arches, in a Mediterranean echo of the slender forms of northern Gothic art.

Porxos d'en Xifré
(Xifré Porches)

After the "discovery" of America, many Catalans travelled there to seek fortune. Many succeeded as commercial agents or in small businesses and returned to Barcelona. These *indianos*, as they were called, became influential because of their ostentatious display of wealth. They were wont to erect magnificent private homes in the city or their native villages. This was the case of **Josep Xifré i Cases** (1777-1856), a merchant who amassed a great fortune in Cuba and returned home to find himself the richest man in Barcelona. The complex of neo-Classical buildings with arcades that he built is now a labyrinth of busy shops.

Take Avenguda del Marquès de l'Argentera.

Duana Nova
(Aduana Nueva)

The building destroyed by fire in 1777 was rebuilt with neo-Classic and Rococo touches. Since 1902, it has been the headquarters of the Prefecture.

Estació de França*

Built in 1929, this huge **iron structure** crowned by glass roofing is, as the name would suggest, a terminal for trains to France. It also stages important cultural events, such as the Annual Comics Fair.

Parc de la Ciutadella*

After the long period of resistance when Barcelona was under siege by Philip V (1714), the Bourbon King commissioned a formidable fortress, La Ciutadella, to intimidate and watch over people. In 1715, construction of the buildings and ramparts began, using innovative French techniques, and requiring the demolition of more than one thousand houses in the Ribera neighbourhood. This fishermen's' district, densely populated and a centre of business, was razed nearly to the last inch. The fortress became, like Montjuïc castle, a symbol of repression in the eyes of the people. One of the

J. Balanya/MICHELIN

Parc de la Ciutadella

main demands of the Catalan nationalist movement of the 19C was its destruction. The fortress was finally dismantled after the 1868 revolution and a public park was created on the site. In 1888, triumphantly, the Universal Exhibition was held there.

The monumental access to the park, **passeig de Sant Joan**, was designed as a long avenue leading to the centre of town and into the heart of the old citadel. This straight line goes through the entrance at the **Arc de Triomf**, built for the Exhibition and recently restored.

Inside the park, there are two **museums** (of zoology and a geology) and the city **zoo**. *(see "Other museums and sights of interest")*.

Castell dels Tres Dragons** – This monumental building ("Castle of Three Dragons") in iron and red brick, in Catalan neo-Gothic style, was designed by Domènech i Montaner in 1887 to be used as a restaurant for the Universal Exhibition. Outside, note the large windows of Gothic inspiration, the Roman-style crenels and the ceramic panels painted with allegorical figures and fantastic images. Inside, you will find the **Museu de Zoologia,** a relentlessly old-fashioned collection of stuffed creatures in glass cases.

Hivernacle i Umbracle – These two buildings face each other. The greenhouse is an example of iron and glass architecture typical of the early 20C. The conservatory has an extensive collection or tropical plants. In addition to the exotic flora, white-clothed tables and bow-tied waiters serve tropical afternoon meals or drinks. In the summer months, there is jazz and classical music at night.

Between the two, the **Museu Martorell de Geologia** *(☎ 93 319 68 95)* is the oldest in the city (1882). Geologist Francesc Martorell donated his collection to found it. There are scale models and an interesting collection of minerals and palaeontology that includes fossilized plants and animals more than 120 million years old from Spain and other parts of Europe.

Waterfall* – This impressive waterfall was designed by Gaudí when he was still a student. The small nearby lake is suitable for leisurely boat rides.

Plaça de Armes – The landscaped area in the centre of the park is the only place you'll see vestiges of the old citadel: the **arsenal**, a Baroque building (now seat of the Catalonian Parliament), the Governor's Palace (now a school) and the chapel.

Josep Llimona's sculpture *Desconsol* (1907), a woman collapsed in despair, is centered in a peaceful glass-like pond in the main courtyard.

Return by Avenguda del Marquès de l'Argentera as far as Pla del Palau and turn left on Passeig Joan de Borbó.

alburet/MICHELIN

Parque de la Ciutadella

La Barceloneta*

After the demolition of most of the La Ribera, the military engineer J. Martín de Cermeño planned the construction of a new neighbourhood that became know as La Barceloneta.
At the beginning of Passeig Joan de Borbó stands the **Palau del Mar**, a group of buildings dating from the early 20C that once housed the warehouses for the Port of Barcelona. Today, one of the most important tenants is the **Museu d'Historia de Catalunya** *(see "Other museums and sights of interest")*.
This sector, made up of 15 long streets bisected by 15 short streets, is inhabited by fishermen, dockers and others who work on the waterfront.
The **Sant Miquel del Port*** church, an elegant building from 1753, dominates the Plaça de la Barceloneta, and it is the hub of this neighbourhood that extends from the Parc de la Ciutadella to the sea.
From the **torre de Sant Sebastià,** a **cable car** and a **gondola** go up to the Miramar gardens, 80m above sea level, on the side of Mount Montjuïc. A ride up is a great way to take advantage of the **perspective**** on Barceloneta and the wharfs.

Vila Olímpica*

(Olympic Village)

Barceloneta is a neighbourhood full of old-fashioned charm; by contrast the Vila Olímpica is one of the most modern, well-developed sections of the city. Built on the waterfront zone known as El Poblenou to house the 15 000 athletes who participated in the 1992 Olympic Games, the development has brought new energy to the whole waterfront area.
The development project is the work of the architects **Martorell**, **Bohigas** and **Mackay**, and the different apartment blocks were handled by local architects who submitted their ideas in a special competition organised by the FAD (Decorative Arts Foundation).
In addition, la Vila Olímpica has lovely gardens with contemporary sculptures, pleasant, wide avenues and great shopping.
The new **marina****, the work of the engineer J.R. de Clascà, has become one of the city's favourite recreation areas. In addition to the improved beaches of El Poblenou **(Bogatell, Somorrostro, Nova Icària)** there are many outdoor cafés, bars and restaurants that make this popular district colourful and lively until the wee hours of morning. Among the buildings in the area are two towers, 15m high. The skyscrapers are a symbol of modern Barcelona.
The first tower is the **Hotel Arts Barcelona, part of the** Ritz-Carlton group. Designed by a group of American architects, it has an iron structure lending an air of solidity, yet also manages to achieve a graceful outline.

Malburet/MICHELIN

Vila Olímpica

J. Pareto/TOURISME DE LA CATALOGNE

Puerto Olímpico

La **Torre Mapfre**, designed by Íñigo Ortiz and Enrique León, is also 44 storeys high, but looks very different, thanks to the glass façade.

From atop the towers, the **view**★★★ is marvellous; in fine weather, it is possible to see the island of Majorca on the horizon.

La Ribera★

This itinerary takes you through the old quarter of la Ribera, one of the most prosperous sectors of Barcelona from the 13-18C. This historic walk is not only a glimpse into the pre-industrial past of the city, but also shows the confrontation of two essential worlds in the history of Barcelona: merchants and traders, whose great houses were mostly built in the part of la Ribera closest to the sea, and craftsmen, whose guilds met in the upper part of the same district. Although the guilds have all but disappeared today, many of the street names in the upper part of town recall their presence there.

Carrer Montcada★★

Maritime trading played a fundamental role in the history of the city. In the 13-14C, Barcelona's ships dominated trading in the western Mediterranean, especially around the Balearic Islands, Sardinia, Sicily and southern Italy.

Traders' families had acquired a great social prestige and formed a solid oligarchy that controlled the city until very recently, and Carrer de Montcada was the place to see and be seen for this new social class. Indeed, symbolic of the great maritime expansion of Catalans in the Mediterranean, the street owes its name to the powerful, noble family **Montcada**. The private homes and aristocratic mansions date mostly from the late Middle Ages. The street follows a path from the city centre to the port, formerly Carrer "Vilanova del Mar".

Palau Berenguer d'Aguilar★ – The first of the mansions on the itinerary is at no 15. Cross Carrer dela Princesa (the first street in the city to paved), to admire this magnificent residence. Renovated in the 15 and 18C, it still has a many features typical of medieval architecture in Barcelona as expressed in aristocratic dwellings, inspired by the mansions of Italian traders.

The stone and brick façade is imposing and spare of embellishments, save the decoration around the windows on the lower floors. The wrought-iron balconies were added later. The **central patio★**, with a stairway leading to the upper level, or *planta noble*, has open arcades, decorative mouldings and a display of different utensils (jars for oil, wine and water) that recall that the owners made their wealth in trade.

This mansion, the home of **Baron Castellet** (n° 17) and **Palau Meca**, a Baroque building at n° 19 now house the **Museu Picasso** *(see "Museums and sights of interest")*.

Palau del Marquès de Llió (n° 12) – Like the Palau Berenguer d'Aguilar, this residence is also typical of the Catalan Gothic style: central patio, stairway to the *planta noble*, ground floor reserved for utility rooms. The characteristics that differ from the original style are the result of 18C modifications.

The upper section of the façade has on open gallery that may have been used to spread out wool. The narrow windows are typical of the period. On the patio, you can relax at a pleasant bar-restaurant. The building is the home of the **Museu Tèxil i d'Indumentària** (Textile and Clothing Museum - *see "Other museums and sights of interest"*).

Nearby, the elegant Palau Nadal, a 12C building, restored in the 18C, houses the Museu **Barbier-Mueller,** devoted to pre-Columbian art *(see "Other museums and sights of interest")*.

Casa Cervelló-Giudice (n° 25) – This house, an example of 15C Catalan Gothic architecture (patio with stairway to the *planta noble*, was the home of the Cervelló family and later, the Giudices, bankers from Genoa. The **Maeght Gallery** is located here.

Palau Dalmases (n° 20) – This manor, among the others, has the greatest original decorative wealth. The first building (witness the vaulted chapel in late medieval style) was remodelled at the end of the 17C, when the Dalmases family purchased it.

The transformation of the building was closely supervised by Dalmases, a textile manufacturer who had made a fortune in the trade. They designed the splendid friezes decorating the rail of the covered stairway leading up from the patio. It is adorned with twisted and grooved columns and intertwining trellises, and features subjects from mythology such as the Rape of Europe and Neptune's Chariot. Currently, part of the building is reserved for exhibits organised by the **Sala Montcada**.

J. Balanya/MICHELIN

Calle Montcada

At the end of Carrer Montcada, the east end of the church of Santa Maria del Maris on the right and the Passeig del Born on the left.

Iglesia de Santa María del Mar**

"Santa Maria!" was the battle cry of the Catalan army and navy. Jaime I swore that after the conquest of Majorca, he would build a cathedral in honour of the Virgin Mary. One hundred years later, when Catalan ships dominated the Mediterranean, the church of Santa Maria del Mar was built. If the Cathedral was the centre of the old Duchy, Santa Maria held pride of place in the district of merchants and sailors, the city's new heroes.
Built in the 14C with unusual speed for a building of such size, it quickly became the spiritual centre of the neighbourhood. It sometimes referred to as "the cathedral of la Ribera", for the sailors living in la Ribera, although of modest means, gave as much as they could to create a place of worship that would rival that financed by the bourgeoisie.
The result of their efforts came to be this marvellous church, whose harmony and elegance of form and proportion are celebrated by architects and artists around the world.

Exterior** – This is one of the few Catalan Gothic churches where we can admire a completely finished exterior. The three façades – the main one on Plaça de Santa Maria, the second on Carrer de Santa Maria and the third on Passeig del Born – are representative of Catalan Gothic: emphasis on horizontal forms, massive buttresses, plain surfaces and octagonal pillars.
The main façade is a wonder to observe. Decorated with statues of Saints Peter and Paul, the tympanum bears a large sculptural group. The outstandingly beautiful rose window (15C), in the Flemish Gothic style, is flanked by two bell towers with octagonal bases.
The church extends along Carrer de Santa Maria, where another entrance is located. From this side of the church, you can appreciate the gargoyles and buttresses, the outside faces of the windows and the overall monumental design.
The door that leads to the apse (the usual entrance), on Passeig del Born, is Gothic in style, although it was built in 1542.
Interior*** – The striking beauty of this prodigious work of architecture is immediately apparent upon entering the church. Santa Maria del Mar is the sum of the two most successful achievements of

MATHEMATICS AT THE SERVICE OF HARMONY

The harmony of Santa Maria del Mar arises from precise calculation: the side aisles measure 6.5m, which is half the width of the central nave. The 13m width of the central nave makes it the widest Gothic church in the world. The total width is equal to the height of the side aisles and the difference between this height and the height of the central nave is equal to the width of the side aisles. Between the buttresses, chapels are set in the side aisles in groups of three.

J. Malburet/MICHELIN

Catalan Gothic: pure form and great volume.
Instead of adopting the usual structure of corridors placed side-by-side, the architect designed the church as a "hall", where the three naves, almost identical and very high, are separated by slender, soaring octagonal pillars. The result is an impression of lightness, with the inner supports thus reduced to their simplest expression.
The main altar is surrounded by a curious cluster of columns that meet to form a ribbed vault.
The unequalled geometric purity of the church interior is the result of architectural genius. The dimensions create an ineffable sensation of peace and light. To cast your eyes upward is to discover a troubling perspective that incites immobility and introspection. At night, the sensation is even more pronounced.
Although the anti-clerical revolt of 1936 caused the destruction of the interior decoration, there are still stones in the nave with inscriptions associated with the world of sailors and the sea and ocean trade. The main altar is surmounted by a votive sculpture of a 15C ship, set at the feet of a Virgin and Child.

Interior of the church of Santa María del Mar

Mercado del Born

From the 13-18C, the centre of the city was Passeig del Born; later it became La Rambla. The noble families living on Carrer Montcada followed the movement and enjoyed the legendary tournaments of Knights – "born" means tournament – that were held in this popular quarter, along with many other traditional festivities.

At the end of the promenade, where the local bazaar offered leather goods, Josep Fontseré (1874) designed a more formal market space. The metal structure is one of the first examples of industrial architecture in Spain. While renovation works were underway, significant Roman vestiges were uncovered. Many new shops have enlivened the surrounding neighbourhood of late.

Montjuïc★

The "Mount of the Jews", 173m above the port, was a strategic military position in the Middle Ages.
Towards the end of the 18C, the strange shapes of the rocks on Montjuïc – many buildings in Barcelona were built with stone from the quarries there – were a source of inspiration to artists and engravers. The Universal Exhibition of 1929 transformed the mountain, whose sloped were tamed into gardens, following the plans of the French landscape artist Forestier, assisted by Nicolau Rubió i Tuduri. In ad-

J. Malburet/MICHELIN

dition to the gardens, buildings were erected, and these were renovated on the occasion of the 1992 Olympic Games

The Montjuïc district has many points of interest, including two of the city's main museums: the **Museo Nacional d'Art de Catalunya (MNAC)** and the **Fondació Miró** *(see "Main museums")*.

You can reach the area by the funicular railroad from the port or from any of the streets that lead off the Avinguda del Paralelo and cross Poble Sec. It is also accessible from the industrial park on the Southwest side of the mountain.

At the foot of Montjuïc, between Plaça d'Espanya and the sea, the old industrial district known as **Poble Sec**

Plaça d'Espanya

can be recognized by the tall chimneys of the FECSA power plant. This district is bordered by the **Avinguda del Paralelo**, so-called because it runs exactly along the parallel 41° 44' North. In the early 20C, the avenue was lined with theatres, cabarets and music halls, and sometimes called the Montmartre of Barcelona.

Plaça d'Espanya and Fair Grounds

For **Plaça d'Espanya**, the architect Josep Maria Jujol designed a large fountain at the centre of the square. His modernist style is clearly influenced by Gaudí, with whom Jujol frequently collaborated on projects like the Casa Milà and Park Guëll. The Spanish sculptor Miguel Blay Fabregas created the sculptures adorning the fountain.

A wide avenue, the Avinguda de la Reina María Christina, is flanked by two towers and leads to the Magic Fountain and the Palau National at the Montjuïc. The avenue is often used for trade fairs.

The 47m high towers are modelled on the Campanile di San Marco in Venice. They were built by Ramon Raventós for the 1929 Exposition. One of the most famous constructions made for the occasion is the **Pavelló Mies van der Rohe**** (☏ *93 426 20 89*), designed by the famous architect to represent Germany. Considered to be a seminal example of modern architecture, the Pavilion contained the so-called Barcelona chair, also by van der Rohe, a custom design created for the King and Queen of Spain.

The **Palau Nacional**, a monumental edifice built for the same Exhibition, now serves as the **Museu Nacional d'Art de Catalunya***** *(see "Main museums")*. The esplanade in front of the museum offers a great view of the city, the Plaça d'Espanya and the Fair Grounds.

The **Font Màgica** or Magic Fountain was also part of the 1929 project. Designed by the engineer Carles Buigas (son of the artist who deisgned the monument to Christopher Columbus), it is made of cascades and fountains falling from the Palau National and the Plaça d'Espanya at the foot of the hill. It was originally intended to show people what could be achieved with filtered electrical light. After many years of disuse, the fountain was restored for the 1992 Olympic Games. During summer evenings, when the fountain is activated, it attracts hundreds of visitors who watch the 15-minute spectacular display of light, water and music. The illuminated Palau National provides a beautiful background.

Anella Olímpica* (Olympic Park)

Built as a venue for the sporting events of the 1992 Olympic Games, this huge complex occupies a wide esplanade situated high up on the mountain. Basically, it consists of the **Olympic**

J. Pareto/TOURISME DE LA CATALOGNE

Palau Sant Jordi

Stadium* *(☎ 93 426 20 89)*, with its 1929 façade and fully renovated interior, and the nearby **Palau Sant Jordi**** *(☎ 93 426 20 89)*, a modern sports centre designed by the Japanese architect Arata Isozaki, housed under a large metallic structure.

The **telecommunications tower** commissioned by Telefónica, the work of Santiago Calatrava, offers a pleasing combination of modernity and aesthetics.

Galería Olímpica – *☎ 93 426 06 60*. This gallery commemorates the 1992 Olympic Games: it displays medals won by Spanish athletes, detailed photographs of sporting events which were particularly dramatic that year, and a host of miscellaneous objects associated with the history of the Olympic movement.

Poble Espanyol*
(Spanish Village)

Access from Avinguda Marqués de Comillas. ☎ 93 508 63 00.

This "architectural synopsis" is meant to show the different forms of regional architecture in Spain. It was built by Miquel Utrillo and Xavier Noguès for the 1929 Exhibition.

The Plaza Mayor, with wide arcades, is the scene of folkloric festivities, and the centre

J. Malburet/MICHELIN

Poble Espanyol

of activities. A Majorcan market, a Baroque façade from Valencia, a Galician house or a Castilian square ... all find a place in this panorama of Spanish architecture. The remarkable **Barrio Andaluz** (Andalusian quarter), where the bright colours of geraniums and carnations stand out against the white walls of the houses transports the visitor. Visitors can taste different regional dishes, buy arts and crafts and stay on for a night of barhopping.

Colección de Arte Contemporáneo* – This museum displays the private collection of Fran Darrel, which includes painting, sculpture, engravings, drawings and ceramics. Many great Spanish artists from the 1950s to today are represented (Tàpies, Saura, Equipo Crónica, Chillida, Rafols Casamada, Mompó, Broto, Barceló, to name a few), as well as Picasso, Dalí and Miró.

Following along the Avinguda Marqués de Comillas, turning left out of the Poble Espanyol, you will see **Plaça de Sant Jordi**, with a magnificent **mirador** and a statue of Sant Jordi (Saint George) by Josep Llimona, executed with the expressivity for which he is famed.

Teatre Grec*

(Greek Theatre)

Based on the Epidaurus model from ancient Greece, this 1929 open-air theatre is set against a rocky backdrop belonging to an abandoned quarry. In summer it hosts dance, concerts and stage performances organised by the **Festival del Grec**.

Museu d'Arqueologia de Catalunya*

☏ *93 423 21 49.*

Catalan archaeology has a great tradition and is responsible for some important discoveries. Through the exhibits on display (implements, ceramics, votive figures, household effects etc), visitors are able to follow distinct periods in history from Palaeolithic times through to the Visigothic era, including the periods of Greek and Roman colonisation. The different objects on display (tools, amphors, mosaics or votive scupturess) are characteristic of each of the periods. The specialized library (40 000 volumes) is a valuable research centre.

Other activities take place here, including an innovative workshop for the blind, where partipants learn to identify artefacts through touch.

Museo Etnológico

☏ *93 424 68 07.*

This museum was built on the site of a small pavilion of the Universal Exhibition. Most of the exhibits held here are temporary, although they generally last a long time. The permanent collection includes works from indigenous African, Australian, Central American and certain Asian peoples. Although there are a few pieces of pre-Columbian origin and some ancient Japanese works, most of the collection consists of works of contemporary culture.

Miramar

This esplanade on the North side of the mountain offers – at night especially – a beautiful panoramic view of the city and port, where the ships' light glitter and reflect in the water. Outdoor terraces invite you to sit and enjoy the Mediterranean climate without being bothered by the heat. A cable car links the mirador to the Saint-Sébastien tower on the port.

Château de Montjuïc

The first castle was built here in 1640. During the War of Spanish Succession, the forces of Philip V defeated Barcelona after 13-month siege. The castle was then destroyed, but rebuilt in the 18C.

The castle, like the fortress, was, until the mid-19C, one of the strategic points of Barcelona's defensive system, yet paradoxically it also provided a point from which the city could be attacked. Espartero did just that in 1842, when he turned the canon on the city. For a long time, the castle was also used as a military prison. In 1909, the teacher and anarchist **Ferrer i Guardi** was executed there, and in 1940 the President of the Generalitat, Luis Companys, met the same fate.

Today it is a place for enjoying fresh air and **exceptional views*** over the port and the city. The **Museu Militar** (Military museum) *(☏ 93 329 86 13)*, has a collection of various arms, flags and uniforms.

J. Malburet/MICHELIN

Main museums

Palacio Nacional de Montjuïc, Museu Nacional d'Art de Catalunya

Museu Nacional d'Art de Catalunya (MNAC)★★★

The museum is housed in the Palacio Nacional that was built for the 1929 World Fair. It is a magnificent display of more than 1000 years of Catalan art, from the 10-20C. In addition to paintings and scultptures, the collection includes drawings, engravings, furniture, ancient coins and photography.

J. Malburet/MICHELIN

VISITING THE MUSEUM

☎ *93 622 03 75/ 76. Closed Mon.*

The highlights of the museum are the remarkable **Romanesque and Gothic collections***** taken from many churches in Catalunya and Aragón.

Romanesque art

In the 12-13C the Pyrenean valleys saw the development of a highly expressive and mature art form.

The frescoes are displayed in chapels and large rooms that evoke the atmosphere of contemporary churches. Clearly influenced by Byzantine mosaics, they are characterised by heavy black outlines, superimposed frieze compositions, lack of perspective and rigidity of stance. However, the addition of realistic or expressive details lend a distinctive Catalan touch to these paintings. Note the 12C frescoes by **Sant Joan de Boí** *(Room II)*

with *The Stoning of St Stephen*, *The Falconer* and *Paradise and Hell*, the late 11C lateral apses by Sant **Quirze de Pedret** *(Room III)*, the **Santa María de Taüll** ensemble (12C), presenting a host of images dominated by a fine *Epiphany* and the paintings from Sant Climent de Taüll *(Room V)* with its remarkable *Christ in Majesty*: the apse is considered to be one of the finest examples of Renaissance painting. Note the deliberate anti-naturalistic approach and the subtle geometry of the drawing.

The **altar frontals** fall into two categories: those painted on a single panel (Iglesia de Sant Martí d'Ix, Catedral de Santa María at La Seu d'Urgell, known as the Apostles' altar front) and those carved in relief (Esterrí de Cardós, Santa María de Taüll).

The museum also presents superb **collections of capitals*** *(Room VI)*, silverware and enamels *(Room XV)*.

The section is completed by the paintings from the chapter house at **Sigena** (1200) *(Room XXI)*, which shows the development of changing styles leading to greater naturalism and less stagnant representations.

Gothic art

This section provides visitors with an overview of Catalan Gothic art during the 13C and 14C. Exhibits include the *Annunciation* by the **Master of Anglesola** *(Room III)*, clearly showing the influence of the French linear Gothic style; the stone retables attributed to **Jaime Cascalls** *(Rooms IV and V)*; the large collection of Catalan international Gothic art *(Room IX)*, with works by the city's most influential artists (**Guerau Gener, Juan Mates, Ramón de Mur, Juan Antigó, Bernardo Despuig** and **Jaime Cirera**); the room dedicated to **Bernardo Martorell** *(Room XI)*, an artist for whom detail and pictorial matrixes were of paramount importance; the famous *Virgin of the Councillors* by **Luis Dalmau** *(Room XII)*; the set of works by the **Master of Seu d´Urgell** *(Room XV)* and, lastly, the section dedicated to funerary sculpture in the 14C and 15C *(Room XVIII)*.

From the Renaissance period, which was late reaching Spain, there are a few Flemish and Italian works as well as paintings by Ayne Bru, Pere Nunyes and Pedro Berruguete that retain certain Gothic features.

Donation Cambó – The works from the **Cambó Bequest** are deserving of special mention because they make up a collection embracing the history of European painting from the fourteenth century up to the beginning of the nineteenth century, and enjoy the privilege of their own, permanent installation at the end of the visit to the Gothic Gallery. There are works from the Zurbarán school (magnificent still life) and paintings by Tintoretto, de Sebastian del Piombo, Quentin

de la Tour (portraits) El Gréco, Rubens, Cranach the Elder, Goya, etc.
Colección Thyssen-Bornemisza – Previously on exhibit at the Padralbes Monastery, it contains 72 paintings and eight sculptures (from the Middle Ages to the 18C) which were part of the large collection (over 800 works) on show at the Museo Thyssen-Bornemisza in Madrid. Among the numerous works with a religious theme, **Fra Angelico**'s magnificent ***Virgin of Humility**** and **Zurbarán**'s *Santa Marina* stand out, as do several paintings of the *Virgin and Child* (B Daddi, 14C and L Monaco, 15C). Another room worthy of special mention is the **Sala de los Retratos** (Portrait Room) that contains some fine examples of various 15C and 18C schools.

17 and 18C works – The first floor is hung with works by great Spanish painters of the period. Among the most remarkable: Zurbarán's *Immaculate Conception*, Velásquez' *Saint Paul*, Ribera's *Martyrdom of Saint Bartholomew.*
19 and 20C works. – From the earlier period, you will see paintings by Fortuny, an artist strongly influenced by Delacroix in regard to his use of colour and choice of subjects. There is also a very fine collection of Modernist works including sculptures, posters and drawings by artists such as Gaudí, Doménech i Montaner, Casas, Rusiñol, Mir et Nonell. Noucentism is also represented with works by Sunyer o Clarà.
The last rooms are devoted to avant-garde art: among other works are sculptures Gargallo and Julio González.

J. Malburet/MICHELIN

Fundació Joan Miró★★★

Joan Miró (1893-1983) was unquestionably one of Europe's leading figures in the field of avant-garde art. His name is closely associated with Palma de Mallorca as well as Barcelona, his native town on which he has clearly left his mark. Examples of his work can be found in many different parts of the city: a ceramics mural at the

J. Malburet/MICHELIN

airport, pavement mosaics on La Rambla, not to mention the famous logo he designed for the savings bank La Caixa, symbolising all its local branches.

Born in Barcelona, Miró spent 1921 and 1922 living in Paris, where he painted **La Masía**, a canvas that prefigured his departure from figurative art. Between 1939 and 1941 he executed **Constellations**, his famous series of 23 panels expressing his horror of the Second World War. The themes illustrated in this series (the night, the sun, women etc) were to become recurring motifs in his later work. Miró's art consists in exploring the many possibilities offered by colours,

People, birds, star by Joan Miró – Fundació Joan Miró

shapes and symbols. His work is a skilful combination of joy and tragedy, enhanced by a strong touch of magic and poetry *(see the video presentation of the artist)*.
Created by Miró in 1971, the Foundation was officially opened in 1976. It is housed in a modern building of harmonious proportions, designed by the architect Josep Lluís Sert, a close friend of the artist whose main concern was to conceive a building that blended in well with the surrounding landscape. The collections, totalling over 10 000 exhibits (paintings, sculptures, drawings, collages and other graphic works), bring together many of Miró's works, the majority of which were executed during the last 20 years of his life.

Visiting the Foundation

☎ *93 443 94 70*. The collection includes more than 10 000 works by Joan Miró (painting, sculpture, drawing, collage and graphic works); the ***Serie Barcelona***, is a set of 50 black and with lithographs depicting the Spanish Civil War.

You can also visit a small exhibition of contemporary art featuring works by artists such as Matisse, Tanguy, Max Ernst, Chillida, Saura, Rauschenberg etc.
Since 1990, the Foundation has provided the opportunity for visitors to admire the ***Mercury Fountain**** by Alexander Calder. Calder designed this fountain, with real mercury, for the Spanish Pavilion at the 1937 World's Fair in Paris. It was in the entrance hall, opposite Picasso's Guernica, also designed especially for the exhibition. Like Picasso's painting, this sculpture is a political statement, protesting Franco's siege of the Almadén mercury mines during the Spanish Civil War. Today the fountain is housed behind glass.
In addition to exhibits on the works of Joan Miró, the Foundation organizes temporary exhibits devoted to 20C art and contemporary artistic creation.
Next to the Foundation lies a small garden of sculptures, presenting the work of young Catalan artists.

Museu d'Art Contemporani de Barcelona (MACBA)★★

Barcelona transformed the old **Barri Chino**, or Raval, source of inspiration for many writers (**Juan Marsé,** Camilo José Cela), into a neighbourhood of modern cultural centres. The popular and slightly sleazy feel of the area was turned on its head with the arrival of spectacular new buildings, the most striking of which is the Museum of Contemporary Art of Barcelona, designed by the American architect Richard Meyer. The huge **building**★★ presents characteristics of the rationalist Mediterranean tradition while also introducing modern elements of contemporary architecture. Two significant works can be seen outside: *La Ola* by Jorge Oteiza and Eduardo Chillida's mural, *Barcelona*.

Visiting the MACBA

☎ *93 412 08 10.* The **permanent collections**★ housed in large, pristine white

J. Pareto/TOURISME DE LA CATALOGNE

MACBA

exhibition rooms, cover the major artistic movements to have emerged in the past 50 years.

Exhibits include works influenced by Constructivism and Abstract art (Klee, Oteiza, Miró, Calder, Fontana), as well as creations by experimental artists (Kiefer, Boltanski, Solano) and names typically associated with the 1980s (Hernández, Pijuán, Barceló, Tàpies, Ràfols Casamada, Sicilia).

There are works from the schools of Constructivism and Abstraction (*Beschwingte Bindungen*, by Paul Klee, two extraordinary mobiles by Alexander Calder, *Concetto Spaziale* by Lucio Fontana, *Femme dans la Nuit* by Joan Miró, *Planos de color con dos maderas superpuestas*, by Joaquín Torres-García and the magnificent variations known as *Desocupación no cúbica del espacio*, by Jorge Oteiza).

There are experimental works (*Réserve des Suisses morts*, by Christian Boltanski, *Das Glab in den Lüften*, by Anselme Kiefer and *Portrait*, by Muntadas); works representative of the 1980s (*Triptych by Granada*, by Joan Hernández Pijuan, *Dues creus negres*, by Antoni Tàpies, *Pintura 2 – hommage to Joan Miró –* by Alberto Refols Casamada, *Black Flower*, by José María Sicilia).

Other important works are *Saison des pluies 2* (1990), by Miquel Barceló, the artist's personal interpretation of rain as a symbol of fertility and a metaphor for regeneration, and *Asociació Balnearia 2* (1987), a monumental sculpture by Susana Solano, contrasting the strength of wrought iron with a pile of tree trunks set against a wall, a statement of the diversity found in nature and the coldness of human construction.

Many temporary exhibits are held here too, as well as conferences, concerts and other activities related to contemporary art. There is a wonderful art library.

Centre de Cultura Contemporània de Barcelona (CCCB)

☏ *93 306 41 00*. The former Casa de la Caridad has absorbed part of the MACBA. the CCCB and the Centro de Estudios y Recursos Culturales.

This busy arts centre is in a building remodelled by the architects Piñón and Viaplana, and features an unusual **patio*** where decorative elements are used in an origanal combination of the traditional – mosaics, silk-screen floral motifs – and the contemporary – a large pane of glass in the centre that offers interesting reflections of the surroundings.

The centre's activities are very diverse. Conferences, courses in contemporary art, temporary exhibits and many other activities related to contemporary art and studies on urban planning.

S. Balcells © CCCB

CCCB patio

Centro de Estudios y Recursos Culturales

☏ *93 402 25 65.*

Also known as the Patio Manning, the cultural resource centre offers a beautiful space for researchers: the interior patio, with two stories, columns and mosaics.

Museu d'Història de la Ciutat★★

The Clariana-Padellàs House (15C), home to the museum, bears the name of a noble family of Barcelona. It was moved, stone by stone, from its original site on Carrer dels Mercaders to Plaça del Rei.

Visiting the Museum

Entrance from Carrer del Veguer. ☎ *93 225 47 00.*

The visit begins with a series of rooms that explain the foundation of the Roman city. A 30-minute film tells the story of Barcelona. Vestiges of the ancient Roman city were discovered underneath the Plaça. A visit to the underground archaeological site 4,000 square metres below the square, which displays remains from the first century BC to the eighth century AD, allows us to find out what the Roman colony was like and to see the Episcopal ensemble of Barcino. The subterranean path leads to the Palau Reial Major *(see below)*.

The Roman city★★★ – In the underground galleries, you can see the Roman and Visigoth vestiges that remain from the embryonic city of Barcelona (4-7C). This unusual promenade below the modern town is a unique experience. You will walk past bits of standing walls, narrow streets, Roman houses and workshops. Clearly visible remains include a shop where foods were preserved, a washhouse, and a wine shop. From the Roman city, visitors pass into two vaulted rooms that were part of the old Palau Condal (palace of the counts of Barcelona). There are sculptures, epigraphs and busts dating from the 1-4C. Two 13C Gothic frescoes were discovered in the Sala Jaime I in 1998.

Palau Reial Major – Initially built in the 11C and 12C, the palace was gradually enlarged over the years until it acquired its present appearance in the 14C. It used to be the official residence of the counts of Barcelona and subsequently that of the kings of Aragón. The façade features huge buttresses linked together by arches. At the back of these arches lies the original Romanesque façade with its trilobate windows and Gothic rose windows.

Capilla de Santa Àgueda★★ – This 14C palatine chapel with a single nave is covered by intricate polychrome woodwork panelling. It houses the **Altarpiece of the Constable★★**, executed by Jaime Huguet in 1465, depicting scenes from the life of Jesus and the Virgin Mary. In the centre, the *Adoration* *of the Three Wise Men* is a masterpiece of pictorial art from Catalunya.

A side staircase leads to the **Mirador del Rei Martí**, a five-storey tower commanding a lovely **view**** of the old city, with the cupola of the Basílica de la Mercè looming in the distance.

Salón del Tinell – This lofty 14C room, 17m/56ft high, is covered with a two-sloped ceiling resting on six vast round arches. According to tradition, it was here that the Catholic Monarchs received Christopher Columbus in 1493 after he returned from his first voyage to America.

J. Malburet/MICHELIN

Capilla de Santa Àgueda

J. Malburet/MICHELIN

Other museums and sights of interest

Cloisters of the Pedralbes Monastery

Eixample

Fundació Arqueològica Clos: Museu Egipci de Barcelona

☎ *93 488 01 88.* Recently installed in a new building, this interesting private museum has about 600 items representing different periods of Egyptian civilisation and a few pieces from Roman times. The collection is arranged thematically. The sarcophagi, mummies and funerary masks are testimony to the importance of the after-life in ancient Egyptian religion. Also on exhibit from the same period: a collection of gorgeous **"Jewellery of the Pharaohs"★**, and everyday objects. A statue of Ramses II and two well-preserved statues from the Ancient Empire are also well worth a look.

Barri Gòtic

Museu Frederic Marès★

Entrance from Plaça de Sant Iu. ☎ *93 310 58 00.* The museum conserves the collection that was assembled by its founder, Frederic Marès, who donated it to the city of Barcelona. Marès (1893-1991), a well-known sculptor, transformed his early fondness for collecting into an untiring and fruitful passion to gather all kinds of objets d'art and objects from everyday life belonging to past centuries that today make up the rich and varied museum collection. There are three clearly differentiated sections: the sculpture collection, the Collector's Cabinet and Frederic Marès' library-studio.

Sculpture Section – This collection mainly gathers together Spanish artistic pieces, from the pre-Roman era to the 20C, among which the pieces from the Middle Ages and the polychrome religious carvings stand out. One of the masterpieces in this section is the relief called *Appearance of Jesus to His Disciples at Sea*, from the monastery of Sant Pere de Rodes. Renaissance and Castilian Baroque sculpture is well represented; there are examples of most of the Spanish schools of sculpture, from the medieval era to more modern periods. Of special note: **Cristos y Calvarios★★**, **Virgin and Child★**, **Santo Entierro★** and the carving of **The Vocation of Saint Peter★**.

In the same sculpture section there is a collection of religious apparel, lace, braid, embroidery and other samples of needlework, and above all, painting, in which the medieval panels stand out.

The iconographic richness of the collection and the diversity of the materials and types of work on display are inherent, and complementary, aspects of the historical approach, in which prominent or anonymous artists introduce visitors to, or further their knowledge of this singular collection of Hispanic sculpture.

Gabinete del coleccionista – The Collector's Cabinet, or the Sentimental Museum, consists of handmade work that shows us objects used in everyday life from the 15-19C.

The Ladies' Quarter is one the most emblematic rooms in the museum, and is a testimony to the world of women in the Romantic period. It displays collections of fans, combs, small boxes, pins, jewels, dress dummies, vases, clothing and other fashion accessories.

The Entertainments Room, with toy theatres, automatons, toys, etc., preserves all the charm and power that bygone ways of enjoyment evoke. All the objects related to 18C leisure-time activities are gathered here.

The Smoker's Room displays a great variety of pipes, objects that attained a high level of refinement both for the quality of the materials used and for their delightful shapes.

Library and studio – This area assembles a group of sculptures by Frederic Marès in his private library-studio. Located on the second floor of the building, the arrangement has hardly been changed since he used it. It was opened to the public on 6 June 1996.

Around la Rambla

Iglesia de Sant Pau del Camp

Access from Carrer de Sant Pau. The year of construction of this Romanesque jewel is not known, but the oldest reference to it dates from the year 912, when the Count of Barcelona Wilfred II was buried here, making it the oldest church in Barcelona. Once part of a Benedictine monastery, it was pillaged by El Mansur and the Almoravides and later burned during the *Setmana Tràgica* in 1908. The plan is cruciform; the façade is decorated with blind arcades set on sculpted bases. Some Visigoth elements are still visible: two capitals in marble supporting imposts with interlacing supporting the archivolt embellished with carvings. A bell tower with openings surmounts the Baroque-style octagonal lantern.

The interior, with a single nave and cradle vaulting, is pure in its proportions. The chapel of the Holy Eucharist, former chapter house, is accessible from the right arm of the transept. The small cloisters (11-12C) are very pleasant, lined with twinned columns.

Iglesia de Santa Anna

Near the Plaça de Catalunya. Closed in by the surrounding houses, this elegant Romanesque church was once part of a monastery; the little cloisters with slender columns are all that remain from the monastery.

Museu de Cera

Access from La Rambla and Passatge de la Banca. ☎ 93 317 26 49. Since 1973, the wax museum has been in this former private residence dating from the 19C. On the façade, next to four original sculptures, you can see Superman and *C3PO*, the android from *Star Wars*. More than 360 figures of famous people from all times, real or fictitious, populate the museum. The cafeteria Bosc de las Fades is worth a look: it is a shadowy cave representing an enchanted forest.

Waterfront

Museu Marítim*

☎ 93 342 99 20. The magnificent shipyards, **Drassanes Reials****, the oldest medieval shipyards still standing in Europe *(see "La Rambla")* provide a splendid home for the museum. The most outstanding exhibition here is a reconstruction of La Galería Real of Don Juan de Austria, a lavish royal galley that served in the battle of Lepanto (1571). Another special exhibit features a map by Gabriel de Vallseca that was owned by explorer Amerigo Vespucci.

© Museu Marítim de Barcelona

Galería Real of Don Juan

The ticket also provides entrance to the ***pailebote Santa Eulàlia***. This three-masted schooner (1918) docks at Moll de Bosch i Alsina, off La Rambla de Mar.

Aquàrium*

☎ *93 221 74 74*. This is one of the largest aquariums in Europe. Twenty tanks contain all species of Mediterranean Sea life as well as tropical specimens. During the visit, you will walk through an underwater tunnel 80m long, surrounded by curious fish (including sharks). A special place is reserved for children, for fun and learning through interactive activities.

Museu de Zoología*

In the Parc de la Ciutadella. ☎ *93 319 69 12*. The zoo has a large collection of species from the animal kingdom. The ground level, where a great whale skeleton greets visitors, is the stage for temporary exhibits. On the floor above, the permanent exhibit is "Sistemática del Reino Animal", with mammals, birds, reptiles, Coleopterans, Lepidoptera and molluscs among others. The room where you can listen to the cries of different animals is entertaining.

Parc Zoológico*

In the Parc de la Ciutadella ☎ *93 225 67 80*. This zoo takes up a large part of the Parc de la Ciutadella, in which animals from all over the world can be seen in their natural environment. A popular dolphin show is held in the Aquarama.

Museu d'Història de Catalunya*

☎ *93 225 47 00*. This museum is housed in the former general stores of the port of Barcelona, a group of buildings that date from the beginning of the century. It provides an insight into the history of Catalunya from prehistory to the present day. A documentary centre (library and audio-visual resources) on the history of Cataluyna is also housed on the premises

La Ribera

Museu Picasso*

☎ *93 319 63 10.* In 1963, the Picasso Museum was inaugurated in the Aguilar Gothic palace. In 1970 the Barcelona City Council enlarged the museum by annexing the Palau del Baró de Balaguer (it was twice called the Baró de Castellet in the past), and later adding the Palau Meca. In 1999, a new museum enlargement was inaugurated with the restoration of Casa Mauri and the Palau Finestres as venues to hold temporary exhibitions. The five palaces mentioned above are the magnificent repositories of the present-day Barcelona Picasso Museum.

The collections of the Picasso Museum reveal, to a large extent, the relations that the artist maintained with Barcelona and depict the key moments of this affinity. As a matter of fact, a large part of present collect comes from the donation that Picasso himself made in 1970 of all his early work, as well as works donated by Jaume Sabartés.

Owing to this, the museum is very rich in regard to work from the formative periods in the life of the artist. The museum possesses an important representation of works from 1917, the year that Picasso met Olga Kokhlova and went to Rome with Diaguilev's ballet company to prepare *Parade*. Afterwards, he would travel to Barcelona to introduce her to his family. Therefore, that year Picasso spent a long period in Barcelona. A group of very important works bears witness to this stay; they mark the transition from Cubism to the reencounter with classicism, favoured by his journey to Italy. Some examples of these are *Harlequin*, Woman with *Mantilla*, *Figure with Fruit Dish* and *Blanquita Suárez*, excellent Cubist pieces, but with more concessions to polychromy and ornamental elements.

The collection is exhaustive up to the Blue Period, of which the museum has a priceless group of works. The end of this period coincides with Picasso's departure to live indefinitely in Paris, in April 1904.

As can be appreciated, the collections in the Picasso Museum have an unquestionable Barcelonan character, and at the same time, have given a marked Picasso character to Barcelona.

Also noteworthy: the section devoted to the artist's youthful works, such as *First Communion* (1896) and *Science and Charity* (1897); the series ***Las Meninas**** of 58 oil paintings, 44 inspired by the famous painting by Velázquez.

Museu Tèxtil i de la Indumentària

☎ *93 310 45 16.* The Textile and Clothing Museum is an institution charged with safeguarding the valuable heritage of material history formed by textiles, tap-

Picasso Museum, patio

alburet/MICHELIN

estries, embroideries, lace, liturgical ornaments, civil dress and accessories, and apparatus for the production of these objects, dating from the early centuries of our era to the present day. In addition to the preservation and study of these materials, the museum seeks to act as a vehicle conveying the creativity that has marked textile and clothing design over the course of history. The museum contains remarkable examples of Coptic and Hispano-Arabic textiles.

Museu Barbier-Mueller d'art precolombí

☎ *93 310 45 16*. This is one of the most important collections of pre-Columbian art in the world. In the elegant Palau Nadal, the collection contains almost 6,000 pieces of tribal and ancient art. Josef Mueller (1887-1977) acquired the first pieces by 1908. Pre-Columbian cultures created religious, funerary, and ornamental objects of great stylistic variety with relatively simple means. Stone sculpture and ceramic objects are especially outstanding. Many exhibits focus on the Mayan culture, the most homogenous and widespread of its time, dating from 1000 B.C. Mayan artisans mastered painting, ceramics, and sculpture. Note also the work by the pottery makers of the Lower Amazon, particularly those from the island of Marajó.

Pedralbes

The former village of Pedralbes – the name derives from the white stones *(pedres albes)* of the mountain – is now a prestigious residential neighbourhood of Barcelona.

Monasterio de Santa Maria de Pedralbes★★

☎ *93 315 11 11*. The convent **church★**, a spacious building with a single nave and side chapels, contains the mausoleum of Queen Elisenda de Montcada. The interior is divided lengthwise into two sections, only one of which is open to visitors. The other, separated by a grill, is reserved for the religious community of Clarissa nuns. On the side façade, the buttresses of the church and the bell tower were an inspiration to the French architect Le Corbusier. To the right, a steep stairway leads to the fortified door of the old convent prison.

Cloisters★ – A magnificent example of 14C Catalan Gothic architecture, the cloisters are on three levels. The two lower levels have pointed arches above grooved columns, surrounding a lovely garden of orange trees and palms. In the gallery, several cells and utility rooms are open to the public.

To the right of the entrance, the Capilla de San Miguel is a small room with interesting **frescoes★★★** (1346) by

Pedralbes Monastery

J. Malburet/MICHELIN

Pedralbes Monastery

Ferrer Bassa. This artist, trained at the Italian school known as "Trecento", created work that harmoniously combined the meticulous nature of the Sienna school and the volumes of Tuscan masters. In the upper area, scenes from the Passion of Christ surround a composition of Calvary; the delicate paintings of the Virgin Mary are the most beautiful.
In the former dormitory of the Clarissa sisters and in the Queen's room, you can see some of the convent's treasures.

Palau de Pedralbes

Access by Avinguda Diagonal. ☎ 93 280 16 21.
Less striking but still of interest is the Royal Palace of Pedralbes built in Italianate style in 1919-29 for Alfonso XIII onto an existing building which was formerly the home of Gaudí's patron Eusebi Güell. Its public rooms are now devoted to two collections, the Museum of Decorative Arts and the Ceramics Museum.
Museu de les Artes Decoratives★ – The collection includes an interesting assembly of household items from the Middle Ages to the early industrial age. Chests, desks, chairs, lamps, cupboards and bottles, among the many objects, create a picture of the evolution of society.
Museu de la Ceràmica – The ceramics collection includes Spanish pieces from the 13C to the present. Of particular interest are the items from Cataluyna, Valencia and Alcora (18-19C)
In the contemporary section, there are works by Llorens Artigas, Picasso and Miró.

Outskirts of Barcelona

Museu de la Ciència

At the foot of Tubidabo. ☎ *93 212 60 50.* Ideal for young visitors, this modern museum in a 20C building is devoted to science and seeks to make it accessible through fun activities. The main attractions are Foucault's pendulum, which demonstrates the rotation of the earth, the planetarium and the rooms devoted to optics, perception and weather. Visitors can carry out experiments, some of them quite surprising, such as the high-tension workshop, where a match seems to light itself or you can make your hair stand on end!

Teatre Nacional de Catalunya

South of Plaça de les Glòries Catalanes. The building that houses this modern theatre, designed by Ricardo Bofill, is a synthesis of modern and classic architecture. The entrance is a glass vestibule that is like a greenhouse, full of palm trees and other plants. The main hall, where the headline performances are given, has the form of a classic amphitheatre. The decoration is elegant. The smaller stage, also remarkable, is used for other performances on the schedule (dance, music, etc).

Auditori – Part of one of Barcelona's most important cultural facilities, along with the Teatre Nacional de Catalunya *(across the street)*, the auditorium was designed by Rafael Moneo. The architecture relies on pure lines and the modern facilities make it an excellent venue for musical events.

J. Malburet/MICHELIN

Directory

Bird market

Transportation

Recent improvements have made it much easier to get around Barcelona. A ring road of 40km now circles the city, relieving traffic congestion in the centre.

Aeropuerto – 18km/11mi from the city centre.

– Can be reached by **local train** *(tren de cercanía)* every 30min from 6am to 10pm, from the airport to Plaça de Catalunya (23min); or by the bus service from the Plaça de Catalunya and Plaça de Espanya, departing every 15min from 6am to 12pm. (30 min).

– By **taxi**, the fare from the city centre will be approximately €25.

Taxis – The city's black and yellow taxis are an efficient, inexpensive way of getting around the city. You can catch one at a taxi rank or flag one down.

Transportes públicos – The prices and the hours of operation make public transportationthe most sensible to get around town.

The metro, the Chemins de fer de la Generalitat de Catalunya, the "Tramvia Blau" (tram in the upper part of the Diagonal), and city buses make it easy to get from any one part of town to another. Many stations are equipped to meet the needs of persons of reduced mobility: information ☎ 93 412 44 44.

Metro – *Metro stations are shown on the maps in this guide*. For further **information:** ☎ 93 318 70 74 or visit *www.tmb.net*. The network consists of six lines: L1 (Feixa Llarga/Fondo), L2 (Paral.lel/Pep Ventura), L3 (Zona Universitària/Canyelles), L4 (Trinitat Nova/La Pau), L5 (Cornellà/Horta), L11 (Trinitat Nova/Can Cuiàs). It is open 5am-12pm Mon-Thu; 5am-2am Fri, Sat and days preceding public holidays. Trains every 5 to 9min, depending on the line.

Tickets and cards: Metro tickets and cards can also be used on buses, the "Tramvía Blau" (a tourist tram in the Diagonal section of the city) and train services operated by Ferrocarriles de la Generalitat de Catalunya. In addition to single tickets, multi-journey cards *(abonos)* are also available. These include the **T-10** (valid for 10 trips), **T-DIA** (unlimited travel for one day), **T50-30** (for 50 trips in 30 days) and the **T-MES** (unlimited travel for one month).

City buses – the network includes 80 lines covering different parts of town. Some lines operate until 5am. Metro tickets are valid on the bus.

Some useful lines for tourists:

– 25 from the Santa Creu hospital and la Sagrada Familia to Parc Güell.

– 24 between Parc Güell and Passeig de Gracia (La Pedrera).

Funiculars – **Funicular de Montjuïc**: Paral.lel / Parc de Montjuïc; **Funiculaire du Tibidabo**: Plaça del Funicular / Tibidabo; **Funiculaire de Vallvidriera** Peu del Funicular / Vallvidriera Superior.

Tourist attractions:

Téléphérique – Teleférico de Montjuïc (cable car): closed for work, should reopen in 2006.

Bus Turístic – This excellent service offers visitors a variety of bus itineraries throughout the city (3 itineraries, 40 stops). Daily departures from Plaça de Catalunya starting at 9am.

Boat trips – The company **Las Golondrinas** organises trips around the port (approx 35min) as well as excursions by catamaran (1hr 30min). Departures from Portal de la Pau, opposite the Columbus monument. ☎ 93 442 31 06 or visit *www.lasgolondrinas.com*

Car rental

AVIS – ☎ 902 13 55 31, *www.avis.es*

BUDGET – ☎ 901 20 12 12, *www.eurorenting.org/budget/*

EUROPCAR – ☎ 93 439 84 03. *www.europcar.es*

HERTZ – ☎ 902 40 24 02, *www.hertz.es*

ATESA – ☎ 93 323 07 01

Trains – The suburban lines from la Renfe are another alternative for visiting the outskirts of Barcelona , including Maresme (Mataró, Canet, Calella, etc.), la Costa Daurada (Sitges) or inland towns (Vic). Information: www.renfe.es

S. Ollivier/MICHELIN

Park Güell

DIRECTORY

Sightseeing

Combined tickets and discounts – Three cards give different reductions.

– **Barcelona Card** (1-5 days): unlimited transport, discounts ranging from 20 to 100% in museums, and other reductions for shows and in shops and restaurants. On sale at the city's tourist offices: Plaça de Catalunya, Plaça de Sant Jaime, Sants station, Airport, etc. For further information: ☎ 906 30 12 82 or visit *www.barcelonaturisme.com*

– **Articket**: (valid for three months; €17) entrance to six attractions: the MNAC, the Fundació Joan Miro, the Fundació Antoni Tàpies, the CCCB, the Centre culturel de la Caixa, the MACBA and the Espace Gaudí. ☎ 902 101 212. *www.telentrada.com*.

– **Multiticket de la Ruta del Modernismo** gives access to several emblematic sights of the Modernist movement, with a 50% discount on entrance price. Information at the Casa Amatller, ☎ 93 488 01 39.

Barcelona en la red – *www.bcn.es* : official city site, in Catalan, Spanish and English.

www.barcelonaturisme.com : Tourist Office site, in Catalan, Spanish, French and English.

www.gencat.es : Generalitat site, in Catalan, Spanish, French and English

http://barcelona.lanetro.com/; general information on Barcelona.

www.barcelonastyle.com: information on cultural activities, recreation and nightlife.

www.timeout.com/barcelona/index.html : all kinds of information, in English only.

www.guiadelociobcn.es : complete weekly programme of movies, shows, exhibits, etc, in Spanish.

Publicaciones – The weekly *Guía del Ocio* has the programme of cultural events in Barcelona and Catluyna (available at all news stands). The Cultural Institute publishes la *Guía de los Museos de Barcelona*, a quarterly with complete information on exhibits, opening hours, prices, etc. It is available at the airport and Tourist Offices, along with other official publications for tourists.

Opening times for museums and monuments – Most are open daily except Monday.

Useful phone numbers

Information (calling from Barcelona) – 010; (outside Barcelona) – 932 388 091

Emergency – 112

Medical emergency – 061

Chemists rota – 934 810 060

National Police – 091

Municipal Police – 092

Trains – Renfe (international lines) : 902 240 202. Estació de Sants : 934 903 851; Estació de França: 934 963 464 ; Estació de Passeig de Gràcia: 934 880 236.

Taxis – Radio Taxi Barcelona: 933 581 111 ; Radio-Taxi: 933 033 033.

Post Office – 933 183 831

Airport – 932 983 838

North Barcelona coach station (buses) – 902 303 222

Sea port – 933 068 800

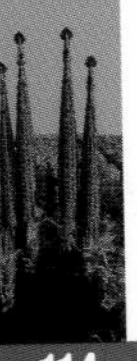

Where to eat

All of these establishments have been selected for their location, comfort, value for money, charm, ambience or unique atmosphere. Prices are given for one economical meal and one meal ordered à la carte. The establishments fall into three categories:

- Budget: under 15 €
- Moderate: between 15 € and 30 €
- Expensive: more than 30 €

Ca l'Estevet – *Valldonzella, 46 (Ciutat Vella) - Universitat - pl. Universidad – 93 302 41 86 - closed Sun and public hols - – €8,30/30.* A small, family-run restaurant with a friendly atmosphere, decorated with attractive *azulejos* and photographs of famous people.

La Provença – *Provença, 242 (Eixample) - Provença – 93 323 23 67 - - €21/25.* In the Eixample district, just a stone's throw from the Passeig de Gràcia. A pleasant restaurant with cheerful, tasteful, decor, serving a good range of regional cuisine.

7 Portes – *Passeig d'Isabel II, 14 (Ciutat Vella) - Jaume I – 93 319 30 33 - - €22/30.* This well-known restaurant, popular with tourists, dates from 1836. It specialises in rice dishes, although the menu also contains a range of traditional dishes. Open until very late.

Agua – *Passeig Marítim de la Barceloneta, 30 (Vila Olímpica) - Barceloneta – 93 225 12 72 - closed at Christmas - - €20/37.* A spacious restaurant with designer furniture and African sculpture. Its terrace, always crowded in summer, is the perfect spot for a quiet dinner by the sea. Mediterranean cuisine and good paellas.

Agut – *Gignàs, 16 (Ciutat Vella) - Jaume I – 93 315 17 09 - closed Sun evening, Mon and in Aug - Resercations advisable – €23/31.* A good location in a narrow street between via Laietana and Avinyó, and close to the Moll de la Fusta. Agut has been serving traditional Catalan cuisine for over 75 years. The pleasant environment is enhanced by the white tablecloths, office-style chairs, and wood panelling on the lower part of the walls.

El Tragaluz – *Passatge de la Concepción, 5 (Eixample) - Diagonal - 93 487 06 21 - closed 1st Jan, Sat and in Aug - €20/48.* This elegant restaurant, which has been decorated like a greenhouse, has a glass roof and contains a number of modern design features, as well as a tapas bar and a fast-food dining area.

Comerç 24 – *Comerç, 24 (Ribera) – 93 319 21 02 - closed in Aug and at Christmas – €29/38.* Innovation and new cuisine in this bar and restaurant. Meals serves at the counter, diners sit on stools. Informal and creative cooking. A special menu allows you to taste a little bit of everything.

El Asador de Aranda – *Av. del Tibidabo, 31 (Sarrià) – 93 417 01 15 – closed Sun evening - – around €33.* In the old Modernist house of Frare Blanc, on the hillside of Tibidabo. The dining rooms have old-fashioned charm and suckling-pig is the speciality. Service on the outdoor terrace in summer.

Los Caracoles – *Escudellers, 14 (Ciutat Vella) - Liceu – 93 302 31 85 - caracoles@versin.com - – €30/41.* Founded 150 years ago, this famous restaurant, one of the gastronomic emblems of Barcelona, is located on the corner of Carrers Escudellers and Nou de Sant Franc. The decor here consists of tiled floors, wine barrels, murals and photos. Regional and traditional cuisine.

⊜⊜⊜ **Talaia Mar** – *Marina, 16 (Vila Olímpica) – ☎ 93 221 90 90 - talaia@talaia-mar.es - ▤ – €33/43.* Ultramodern establishment on the Olympic Port, exceptional view of the sea. Creative regional cuisine. Very good wine cellar.

⊜⊜⊜ **Casa Leopoldo** – *Sant Rafael, 24 (Ciutat Vella) - Ⓜ Liceu – ☎ 93 441 30 14 - closed Mon, evenings of public holidays, during the Holy week and in Aug - €40/60.* This classic Barcelona restaurant is decorated with bullfighting mementoes, signed photos of famous customers and a superb collection of bottles. The only downside is the district, which is not the best in the city.

⊜⊜⊜ **Casa Calvet** – *Casp, 48 (Eixample) - Ⓜ Urquinaona – ☎ 93 412 40 12 - closed during the Holy week, three weeks in Aug, Sun and public hols - ▤ - €43/53.* This restaurant is housed inside the former offices of a textile company, in a magnificent Modernist building designed by Gaudí. The decor is dominated by iron beams and wood floors, while the cuisine is based around traditional, yet creative Mediterranean dishes.

⊜⊜⊜ **Via Veneto** – *Ganduxer, 10 (Sants) – ☎ 93 200 072 44 – closed Sat noon, Sun, 3 weeks in Aug - ▤ - €45/58.* A classic: more than 30 year of experience have established the reputation of this fine, popular Catlan restaurant. Belle Époque decoration. Good, varied wine cellar.

⊜⊜⊜ **Roig Robí** – *Sèneca, 20 (Gràcia) – ☎ 93 218 92 22 – closed Sat noon, Sun, 3 weeks in Augu - ▤ – €48/68.* Elegant, modern establishment in a central location, with wicker furniture and wooden floors. The magnificent landscaped terrace is a lovely place to enjoy the regional dishes on a warm night.

⊜⊜⊜ **Neichel** – *Beltran i Rózpide, 1 (Pedralbes) - ☎ 93 203 84 08 – closed Mon, Sun and Aug - ▤ – €57/70.* One of the most refined traditional Catalan restaurants in town, near the Palau Pedralbes. The dishes are a festival for the senses. The modern details and traditional furniture create an elegant atmosphere.

Tapas

In Tapas bars, prices are not always given. Although each establishment is different, they generally offer a choice of items to make up a meal for less than €15.

Irati – *Cardenal Casanyes, 17 (Barrio Gótico) - Liceu – 93 302 30 84* - . Near the Plaça de la Boqueria, one of the busiest areas of town, this tapas bar serves typical Basque dishes (brochettes) at the counter. In the dining room, meals à la carte.

El Xampanyet – *Montcada, 22 (Ribera) - Jaume I - 93 319 70 03 - Closed Sun evening, Mon, evenings of public hols, in Aug and during Holy Week - €6.* Famous for its anchovies and sparkling wine, which gives the bar its name.

Euskal Etxea – *Placeta Montcada, 1-3 (Ribera) - Liceu – 93 310 21 85 - closed Dec, two weeks in Aug and Sun evening* - - . Next to the iglesia de Santa María del Mar. The perfect setting for a glass of *txacolí* (a Basque white wine) and some appetising Basque delicacies.

Cervecería Catalana – *Mallorca, 236 (Eixample) – 93 216 03 68* - . Bar-pub with a relaxed ambience. Classic decoration, mainly in wood. Good choice of attractive tapas to satisfy customers.

J. Malburet/MICHELIN

Plaça del Pi

Where to stay

Finding a hotel in Barcelona can be difficult. Because there are a lot of tourists, prices have gone up, and it is important to book ahead. Be sure to confirm the price when you reserve. In most hotels, prices are higher in season (between spring and fall)

Selected hotels are divided into three categories for all budgets. Unless there is a special note, the prices correspond to tax-exclusive prices for a single room and a double room in season. These hotels have been selected for their location, comfort, character or value for money.

- Budget, under €50
- Moderate, between €50 and €80
- Expensive, over €80

Hotel Condal – *Boquería, 23 (Barrio Gótico) – 93 318 18 82 - 52 rooms €49,60/70,35 -* . Near La Rambla, this small shopping street is a good starting point for visiting the Ciutat Vella. Warm welcome, simple rooms with baths.

Hotel Urquinaona – *Ronda de Sant Pere, 24 (Ciutat Vella) - Urquinaona – 93 268 13 36 - - 18 rooms €59/89,54 - Restaurant €8/15.* Small hotel in the centre with many young clients. The rooms are functional and clean, stucco walls. Modern facilities, Internet room and small breakfast room.

Hostal d'Uxelles – *Gran Vía de les Corts Catalanes, 688 y 667 (next to Plaça de Tetuan) - Tetuan - 93 265 25 60 - www.hotelduxelles.com - 21 rooms €60/90,15 - €7.* Rooms here are in different parts of the authentically charming building, where the modern and the traditional cohabit in harmony. Antique furnishings, attractive baths with typical Andalusian décor. Most rooms have terraces.

Hotel Medicis – *Castillejos, 340 (Eixample) - Hospital Sant Pau – 93 450 00 53 - – 30 rooms €69/96 - €6.* This modern hotel has a reasonable position opposite the Hospital de Sant Pau, near the Sagrada Familia. The rooms are fairly standard but offer good value for money and an alternative for those who prefer to stay outside the Gothic Quarter.

Hotel Ibis Barcelona Meridiana – *Av. Río de Janeiro, 42 (N of'av. Meridiana) – entrance via Passeig Andreu Nin, 9 – 93 276 83 10 - - 143 rooms €79 - €5.* In the new zone, the hotel with classic style has bright, functional rooms, simply decorated. Modern baths.

Hotel Continental – *Rambles, 138-2° (Ciutat Vella) – 93 301 25 70 - 35 rooms €70/100 - €4.* At the top of La Rambla, not far from the famous Canaletes fountain. Each room in this modern hotel has a different style. The use of fabrics and curtains give it a rather "British" allure. Some rooms have microwaves.

Hotel Granvía – *Gran Vía de les Corts Catalanes, 642 (Eixample) - Catalunya - Gran Vía de Barcelona - 93 318 19 00 - - 55 rooms €75/125 - €10.* This impressive residence dating from the last third of the 19C was built as a home for a wealthy banker. Converted into a hotel in 1936, it has managed to retained its seigniorial air. The room rates here are very reasonable given the charming setting.

Hotel Gaudí – *Nou de La Rambla, 12 (Ciutat Vella) - Liceu – 93 317 90 32 - gaudí@hotelgaudí.es - - 73 rooms €115/150 - €9.* Its location opposite the Palacio Güell and the Modernist decor in the reception area recall the artist who has given his name to the hotel. Those rooms with balconies on the upper floors enjoy superb views of the city and the Palacio Güell.

Hotel Hesperia Metropol – *Ample, 31 (Ribera) - Jaume I – 93 310 51 00 - - 68 rooms €135/150 - €8,41.* This pleasant hotel close to the waterfront is situated in a narrow street in the old quarter, between the Post Office and the Basílica de La Mercè. The main feature here is the lobby, built on a covered patio. The guest rooms are comfortable, with the usual creature comforts.

Hotel Rey Juan Carlos I – *av. Diagonal, 661 (Les Corts) – 93 364 40 40 – - 375 rooms €315/420 - €19 - Restaurant €34/ 53.* A modern hotel surrounded by magnificent gardens and a swimming pool, terraces and a jogging path. The foyer is a beautiful, leading to very comfortable rooms. Excellent fitness centre.

Hotel Arts – *Marina, 19 (Vila Olimpica) - Ciutadella – 93 221 10 00 - - 397 rooms €495 - €25,50 - Restaurant around €64.* Barcelona's most luxurious hotel, with an emphasis on modern art and design. Located in the heart of the Vila Olímpica, with every room enjoying impressive views of the city and Mediterranean.

Out on the town

In Barcelona, nights are lively until dawn, especially on weekends. Here are a few suggestions, from classic cafés for quiet conversation to popular discos.

Café de l'Opera – *Rambla dels Caputxins, 74 (Ciutat Vella) - Drassanes – 93 302 41 80 - abre 9-22.* Because of its history, Modernist façade and 19C atmosphere, this café is one of the most famous in the city. Not to be missed!

Café del Sol – *Plaça del Sol (Gràcia) – 93 415 56 33 - open 1pm-2am.* This old café is calm, with a pleasant terrace for enjoying long balmy evenings.

El Paraigua – *Ptge. de l'Ensenyança, 2 (Horta) – 93 302 11 31 - open 8am-2am; bar daily, except Sun, from 6pm.* This unique café is in an old umbrella store. The decoration includes mirrors and modernist furniture. The bar is in a vaulted cellar (1650) and served cocktails to soothing classical music.

Escribà – Rambla de les Flors, 83 – (Ciutat Vella) - *Liceu – 93 301 60 27 - abre 10am-9pm.* A modernist-style establishment (1820) in an old warehouse. The former Casa Figueras was a family affair until 1920. Today, customers enjoy delicious cakes and savoury dishes in the dining room or on the terrace. A good place to stop and take a break when you are exploring La Rambla.

DIRECTORY

Glaciar – *Plaça Reial, 3 (Ciutat Vella) – ☎ 93 302 11 63 – open from 10am.* This popular Barcelona meeting place on Plaça Reial was a favourite with writers and artists in the past. The pleasant terrace is a perfect place to stop for a drink in fine weather.

Mirablau – *pl. del Doctor Andreu (Sant Gervasi de Cassoles) - ☎ 934 18 58 79 - open 11am-5am.* On the hillside of Tibidabo, near the funicular station. The bar is very nice and the terrace has a great view over Barcelona, especially when the lights come on at night.

Pastís – *Santa Mònica, 4 (Ciutat Vella) - Ⓜ Drassanes – ☎ 93 318 79 80 - open Sun-Thu 7.30pm-2.30am, Fri-Sat 7.30pm-3.30am.* This bar has been in operation for more than 40 years. Enjoy an anis-flavoured *pastis* along with music by Jacques Brel, Georges Moustaki or Édith Piaf. Tuesday nights, dance a passionate tango; Sunday French music is scheduled.

Quatre Gats – *Montsió, 3 bis (Ciutat Vella) – ☎ 93 317 40 33 - open Mon-Sat 5pm-2am.* The symbol of Modernist and bohemian Barcelona. This landmark café was a meeting-place for famous artists such as Picasso, Casas and Utrillo. Reasonable lunchtime menu.

Xiringuito Escribà – *Platja del Bogatell (Vila Olímpica-Poble Nou) - Ⓜ Ciutadella-Vila Olímpica – ☎ 93 221 07 29 - open Tue-Thu 11am-5pm, Fri-Sun 9am-11pm.* Facing the sea, in a lovely setting, this establishing has been quenching local thirsts since 1906 and has become an institution in Barcelona, drawing large crowds.en summer. Delicious seafood and local music.

Luz de Gas – *Moll del Diposit (Port-Vell) – ☎ 93 484 23 26 – www.luzdegas.com - open 12am-3am (only from Apr to Sept).* This popular bar offers a choice of seating: the terrace on the wharf or the interior of the wooden boat. Music and dance floor.

Luz de Gas – *Muntaner, 246 (Eixample) – ☎ 93 209 77 11 - www.luzdegas.com - open from 11pm (closed Sun).* This former Belle Époque theatre is now a hip bar. Once a week, live music (country, jazz, soul and salsa).

La Fira – *Provença, 171 (Eixample) – ☎ 933 23 72 71 - Mon-Thu 10.30pm-3am, Sat-Sun 10.30pm-4.30am.* This picturesque establishment is decorated with automatons and fun fair items.

Bikini – *Déu i Mata, 105 – ☎ 93 322 08 00 - Tue-Sun from 11pm.* On Illa Diagonal, this disco is also a concert venue.

Margarita Blue – *Josep Anselm Clavé, 6 (Ciutat Vella) - Ⓜ Drassanes – ☎ 93 317 71 76 – Open Mon-Wed, 11am-2pm; Thu-Fri, 7am-2pm; Sat, 7am-3am.* Margarita Blue's unusual style of decoration (mirrors of all shapes and sizes, weird and wonderful objects and antique lamps) have helped cement its reputation as one of the most popular bars in the city, hosting weekly shows and concerts. If you fancy a bite to eat, the cuisine here is Tex-Mex. Naturally, the featured cocktail is a salty margerita!

London Bar – *Nou de La Rambla, 34 (Ciutat Vella) -* Ⓜ Liceu – ☎ 93 318 52 81 - *Open Tue-Thu and Sun, 7pm-4am; Fri-Sat, 7pm-5am.* A favourite with circus performers when it first opened in 1909. Hemingway, Miró and others also came here to enjoy its lively atmosphere.

Jamboree – *pl. Reial, 17 (Ciutat Vella) - Ⓜ Liceu – ☎ 93 301 75 64 - Open 10.30pm-5.30am.* The place in Barcelona for aficionados of jazz.

La Paloma – *Tigre, 27 (Sant Antoni) - Universitat – 93 301 68 97 - Open Thu-Sat, 6-9.30am and 11.30am-5pm; Sun, 6-9.30am.* One of the most poplar dance halls in Barcelona. Since 1904, the nostalgia has been building up, layer by layer. The live orchestra makes for a pleasant and relaxing change from clamorous discos.

Otto Zutz – *Lincoln, 15 (Gràcia) – 93 238 07 22 - open Tue-Sun 11pm-5am*. A discotheque and concert hall.

Torres de Ávila – *Avenguda del Marquès de Comillas, 25 (Sants - Montjuïc) - Espanya – 93 424 93 09 - Open Fri-Sat, 12.30pm-7am.* This popular venue, refurbished by the designers Mariscal and Arribas, attracts large crowds in summer.

Marina Port Olympic – *Pg. Maritime Port Olympic.* The marina is one of the most animated parts of town. There is something for everyone: (restaurants, pubs, fast foods, cafés, ice cream parlours, and attractive bars — such as the Gran Casino). Among the many discos, the huge Luna Mora is always full.

J. Malburet/MICHELIN

Café Zurich, Plaça de Catalunya

Entertainment

Barcelona has many cinemas and theatres. Films usually start around 4pm and finish about midnight with an extra showing *(extra)* on Friday and Saturday after midnight. There are discounts tickets on certain days of the week (usually Monday or Wednesday). The **Verdi**, **Casablanca** and **Renoir** are well known and generally show first-run films. La **Filmoteca de Catalunya** shows art-house films, with special programmes devoted to well-known filmmakers.

There are many fine theatres in Barcelona. The very modern **Teatre Nacional de Catalunya**, le **Lliure**, le **Poliorama** and le **Mercat de les Flors** are among the most prestigious.

Servicaixa – La Caixa operates machines that list ongoing entertainment and most enable users to purchase ticket.

Music – Big pop concerts are usually held in the **Palau Sant Jordi** *(see p. 81)*, the **Horta** *(see p. 23)*, la **Plaça de Toros Monumental** and le **Sot del Migdia**, in the centre of the Montjuïc Park.

Le **Festival del Grec begins in late June and continues through the fist week of August, involving several theatres, including naturally, the Teatre Grec de Montjuïc**. Le **Festival de Tardor**, a similar festival, though lesser known, is held in the fall.

The **Palau de la Música Catalana** *(see p. 40)*, the **Gran Teatre del Liceu** *(see p. 60)* and the new **Auditori** are the biggest concert halls in Barcelona.

Tibidabo Amusement Park – ☎ *93 221 79 42. www.tibidabo.es.*

532m above sea level in the Collserola mountains, a giant telecommunications towers, designed by Norman Foster, can be seen from many points around town. Inside, there is an unusual museum of automatons *(☎ 93 211 79 42).*

From the park and from the Sacred Heart temple, a popular wedding venue, the **panoramic view★★** over the city, the sea and the surroundings is extraordinary.

Barcelona is a city of shopping and trade *par excellence.* Shops range from quaint 19C boutiques to the chicest of the chic. Department stores are found in the centre, and stay open all day.

Department stores, shopping streets:

L'Illa Diagonal – *Diagonal, 545 (Les Corts).* A mall designed by architects Rafael Moneo and Ignasi de Solà-Morales: it includes a hotel, schools, a conference centre and many bookshops, clothing, gift and accessory shops.

Maremàgnum – *Moll d'Espanya (Ciutat Vella) - ☎ 93 225 81 00.* This vast space offers recreational activities and shopping; the latest fashions and classic couture wear.

Carrer del Pi – *(Ciutat Vella).* Many small, specialized shops: jewellers, gift shops, layettes, unusual greeting cards and more.

Carrer Pelai – *(Ciutat Vella).* A very busy street with a lot of clothing shops, including a branch of the English C&A, a Zara and lots of shoe stores.

Carrer Petritxol – *(Ciutat Vella).* Shops here serve fine arts students and artists; there are also specialised stationery shops, plush toys, and model shops that sell kits for building scale models of some of Barcelona's remarkable buildings.

Carrer Portaferrisa – *(Ciutat Vella).* Youth fashions: jeans, bright colours, and accessories.

Pla del Palau – *(Ribera).* Many house ware shops around Porxos d'en Xifré sell electric appliances at good prices.

Avenguda del Portal de l'Àngel – *(Ciutat Vella).* For seamstresses and decorators, here is the neighbourhood for finding specialised goods including trimmings for interior design.

Plaça Reial – *(Ciutat Vella) - Sun. 9am-noon.* The stamp and coin market is held on this lovely square on Sunday mornings. Other collectors' items: old post cards, pins, telephone cards. Kids enjoy a visit, as there are a lot of items popular with the younger set for trade or sale here.

Crafts:

Art Escudellers – *Escudellers, 23-25 - ☎ 93 412 68 01 – 11am-11pm*. This huge store in the old town covers two floors. The windows show all kinds of ceramics and other crafts from different regions of Spain. The Catalan products hold pride of place, naturally. There is a good choice of tableware, bathroom accessories and garden ornaments. In the basement, there is a special section for the sale of wine and the famous *cava*.

Cerería Subirà – *Baixada de la Llibreteria (Ciutat Vella) – Mon-Fri. 9am-1.30pm, 4-7.30pm, Sat 9am-1.30pm.* Founded in 1761 by Paulí Subirà, this shops sells all sorts of candles. The decoration is 19C, the oldest in Barcelona. Wide range of models and colours.

La Manual Alpargatera – *Avinyó, 7 - Barcelona - ☎ 93 301 01 72 – daily except Sun 9.30am-1.30pm, 4.30-8pm.* This workshop and store specialises in hand-made espadrilles. In operation since the 1940s, its clients have included many celebrities. Traditional and innovative models.

The decoration, making use of typical objects, creates a warm ambience. Will ship abroad.

Art Galleries:

Barcelona's most prestigious galleries can mainly be found in the Carrer Consell de Cent (**Carles Tatché, René Metras, Sala Gaudí**), along the Rambla de Catalunya (**Joan Prats**), on the periphery of the Born market and around the MACBA. The **Galeria Maeght** and the **Sala Montcada** are both located in the Carrer Montcada.

Antiques:

Plaça de la Catedral – *(Ciutat Vella).* A small market with stalls selling an eclectic range of antiques is held here on public holidays.

Plaça Sant Josep Oriol – *(Ciutat Vella).* Mirrors, furniture, paintings and household goods are all on sale at this popular Saturday and Sunday market.

Carrer de la Palla and Carrer Banys Nous – *(Ciutat Vella).* These two streets are well-known for their reputable antique shops.

Bulevard Antiquaris – *Passeig de Gràcia 55 (Eixample).* An area containing over 70 shops selling a range of artwork and antiques.

Museum shops:

Museu d´Art Contemporani de Barcelona – *Plaça dels Àngels, 1 (Ciutat Vella).* Creations by Barcelona's avant-garde artists.

Fondació Joan Miró – *Plaça Neptú (Sants-Montjuïc).* A wide range of items reflecting the beauty of Catalan traditional art.

Museu d´Història de la Ciutat – *Baixada Llibreteria (Ciutat Vella).* A great place to find your perfect souvenir.

Museu Tèxtil i de la Indumentària – *Montcada, 12-14 (Ribera).* Books, posters, accessories and clothing.

Markets:

The Barcelona markets are open from daily from 9am-8pm except for Sundays and holidays.

La Boqueria – *Ramblas 91 (Ciutat Vella).* The central market is in a glass and iron building from the late 19C. The best fresh food market in Barcelona.

Mercat de la Concepció – *Aragó, 313 (Eixample).* This modern market is in a building that has recently been completely restored. Plenty of choice of fresh fruits and vegetables.

Els Encants Vells – *Plaça de les Glòries (Eixample) – Mon, Wed, Fri, Sat.* The traditional flea market, Rastro de Madrid. Take a close look at the merchandise and don't hesitate to bargain.

Mercat de Sant Antoni – *Comte d´Urgell, 1 (Ciutat Vella).* Inside the municipal market of the same name, it is open only on Sunday morning. Paradise for lovers of old magazines, newspapers, comic books, stamps and all sorts of out-of-print books, at low prices.

J. Malburet/MICHELIN

Boquería Market

Fiestas

December 8, la **Fira de Santa Llúcia** is a Christmas fair. You can also find seasonal items in front of la Sagrada Familia.

On January 5 in the afternoon, the Three Kings arrive in Barcelona by boat. After this ceremonial landing, a long parade takes place in the evening along the main streets. Candy is thrown to crowd.

The annual **Carnival** in Barcelona ends with the popular and spirited "burial of the sardine" on Ash Wednesday.

April 23 is the Feast of Sant Jordi (Saint George), the patron saint of Cataluyna. The same day, anniversary of the death of Cervantès, is also the Day of the Book and the Rose (Dia del Llibre i de la Rosa), a special day for lovers to exchange these precious gifts.

May 11, in the Carrer de Le 11 mai, by the Hospital, many vendors sell aromatic and medicinal herbs, honey, preserves, etc. This sale marks the beginning of the la **Fira de Sant Ponç**.

The evening before June 24, the feast of **Sant Joan**, is the *verbena*. This fair is the occasion for firecrackers and pyrotechnics. You will run across many "devils" taking part in the *contrefoc*, a lively fireworks show. The streets are full of people and the fun goes on all night long. Traditionally, it is a night for eating *coca* – a tart decorated with pine nuts, fruit or cream – and drinking *cava*.

September 11 in the national festival of Cataluyna *(Diada Nacional di Catalunya)*.

La **Festa Major** is celebrated in honour of the Our Lady of la Mercé, patron Saint of the city. For one week, there are shows, balls and concerts, many held on the streets. This is the city's most important festival.

Index

Director	David Brabis
Series Editor	Ana González
Editorial team	Grace Coston, Blandine Lecomte
Picture Editor	Geneviève Corbic, Alexandra Rosina
Mapping	Michèle Cana, Daniel Duguay
Graphic Coordination	Marie-Pierre Renier
Graphics	Jean-Luc Cannet
Production	Renaud Leblanc
Marketing	Ellie Danby
Sales	John Lewis (UK), Robin Bird (USA)

Manufacture Française des Pneumatiques MICHELIN
Société en commandite par actions au capital de 304 000 000 €
Place des Carmes-Déchaux - 63000 Clermont-Ferrand (France)
R.C.S. Clermont-Fd B 855 200 507

Dépot légal mai 2005 - ISBN 2-06-711546-4
Printed in France 06-05/1.1

Typesetting: NORD COMPO, Villeneuve-d'Ascq (France)
Printing-binding: POLLINA, Luçon (Francia) - L 96119b

MICHELIN TRAVEL PUBLICATIONS
Hannay House - 39 Clarendon Road - WATFORD, WD17 1JA
☎ 01923 205240 - Fax 01923 205241
www.ViaMichelin.com - TheGreenGuide-uk@uk.michelin.com